WHY NOT UTOPIA?

WHY NOT UTOPIA?

A POLITICAL PLATFORM IN SEARCH OF A PARTY

Jack Moscou

iUniverse, Inc.
Bloomington

Why Not Utopia?
A political platform in search of a party

iUniverse books may be ordered through booksellers or by contacting:

iUniverse
1663 Liberty Drive
Bloomington, IN 47403
www.iuniverse.com
1-800-Authors (1-800-288-4677)

Because of the dynamic nature of the Internet, any web addresses or links contained in this book may have changed since publication and may no longer be valid. The views expressed in this work are solely those of the author and do not necessarily reflect the views of the publisher, and the publisher hereby disclaims any responsibility for them.

Any people depicted in stock imagery provided by Thinkstock are models, and such images are being used for illustrative purposes only.
Certain stock imagery © Thinkstock.

ISBN: 978-1-4759-8852-9 (sc)
ISBN: 978-1-4759-8853-6 (ebk)

Printed in the United States of America

iUniverse rev. date: 06/19/2013

Contents

PART 1 America: Myth and Reality

PART 2 A Contrarian View on Five of the Many Major Problems America faces: Crime, Racism, Foreign Policy, Trade and Immigration.

PART 3   Utopian planning and Capitalist Free Enterprise

PART 4   Imagining Utopia

PART 5   Which Side Are You On?

Acknowledgments

My thanks to family and friends who took the time to read the various drafts of *Why Not Utopia?: A Political Platform in Search of a Party*, for their helpful comments and suggestions.

I would like to extend a special thanks to Ann Voorhees Baker (http://netmarketing-123.com), who guided me through the intricacies of Internet blogging, where I first posted much of the material contained in *Why Not Utopia?* and to Larry Kostoff for his encouragement and invaluable insights. Thanks also to Nikki Nojima Louis for her painstaking copyediting and proofreading.

I would also like to acknowledge Hay House, Inc., Carlsbad, CA for permission to reprint extensively from Chapter Nine (pp.168-170) in *Spontaneous Evolution: Our Positive Future (and a Way to Get There From Here)* by Bruce H. Lipton, Ph.D., and Steve Bhaerman (2009).

Although I am not by nature sentimental, *Why Not Utopia?* is dedicated to my daughters Susan, Jacqueline and Kathy; to my grandchildren Danielle, Gyasi, Marcus, Chi and Sekou; and to the many young people they brought into my life. It is my hope that they will live to see a much better world than the one I have inhabited these past 83 years.

Introduction

When I was a kid growing up in the 1930s and 1940s times were terrible: poverty, war, racism, religious intolerance and the subordination of women were rampant everywhere. But there were also vibrant progressive, liberal, left-wing, radical, socialist and communist movements struggling for goals ranging from reform of capitalism to formation of a utopian society. Depending on one's viewpoint, the labels were either pejorative or a promise of a better future.

With the failure of the Soviet Union's socialist experiment—granted it wasn't socialism but a totalitarian version of state capitalism—and the resultant linking of socialism with economic failure, Orwellian Big-Brother government, the total suppression of individual liberty, and torture as an instrument of state control, everything from reform to revolution fell upon hard times in the public square. Totally unbowed and undeterred by the current conventional wisdom that says only capitalism and "the market" can guarantee economic progress and individual liberty, *Why Not Utopia?: A Political Platform in Search of a Party* will attempt to resurrect the utopian dream of a just and harmonious American society. I have no objection to a just and harmonious world-wide society, but I am writing about America because I was born in it, live in it and it is the country that I know best.

Why Not Utopia? is a revised and extended version of a series of posts published in 2011 in www.bloggingforUtopia.com. Before starting the blog, which is no longer up, I read the 2008 platforms of the Republican and Democratic Parties in order to contrast them with a utopian vision of what might be. Since *Why Not Utopia?* was still a work in progress in the fall of 2012, I also read the 2012 platforms of both parties. Although slightly different from those of 2008, with some additions and some omissions, both were very similar to their respective 2008 platforms. Since I will cheerfully attack the Republicans and gleefully mock the Democrats, I encourage you to read their respective platforms to judge the accuracy and fairness of my comments. Lest I be accused in the pages that follow of being cynical about our two-party system, I quote from President George Washington's Farewell Address in a letter to the American public shortly before his retirement in 1796, warning against the party system.

> It serves to distract the Public Councils, and enfeeble the Public Administration . . . agitates the Community with ill-founded jealousies and false alarms; kindles the animosity of one . . . against another . . . it opens the door to foreign influence and corruption . . . thus the policy and the will of one country are subjected to the policy and will of another.

In *Why Not Utopia?* I bring both a "left" and a "contrarian" perspective—not necessarily in that order—to the current political scene. Some of those perspectives are captured in my opinions listed below:

- Poor people are not middle-class people without money; poor is a whole different country.
- All stereotypes break down on the individual level.
- All generalizations, by definition are at best inaccurate and at worst misleading.
- Left-wing revolutionaries run on a program of free love, yet the first thing they do when they get power is to outlaw sex.
- Capitalism has perfected the technique of oppressing people to the point of driving them crazy and then using their craziness to justify the oppression.
- In a healthy society hardly anything is sick and in a sick society hardly anything is healthy.

Let me add a view expressed by the late economist John Kenneth Galbraith to the effect that there is no problem for which man cannot come up with a rational solution, but not until he's tried every other alternative.

In *Why Not Utopia?* it is not my intention to offer a complete and comprehensive utopian solution to the world's problems but simply to suggest some approaches we might take to create a better society. As for any solutions that I do suggest, I caution the reader that all solutions are, by definition, imperfect, incomplete, and lead to a new set of problems.

PART 1

America: Myth and Reality

People and countries that prefer myths to reality will never be able to find solutions—personal or political— to the problems they face.

THE MYTH OF A HAPPY AND CONTENTED COUNTRY

Both the Republican and Democratic Party platforms are clearly in favor of motherhood and apple pie. However, when you read their respective platforms it is surprisingly obvious that they really do have fundamental philosophical differences. I say "surprisingly" because the constant media noise with its emphasis on the superficial rather than substance, the reduction of political discourse to 30-second sound bites, and the predominant role of slash-and-burn personal attacks, tend to drown out any serious discussion of those differences.

The opening paragraph of the Chairman's preamble to the 2008 Republican Party platform reads: . . . *Devotion to the inherent dignity and rights of every person. Faith in the virtues of self-reliance, civic commitment, and concern for one another. Distrust of government's interference in people's lives.*

In contrast, the opening paragraph of the 2008 Democratic party platform is a laundry list of "feel-good" ideas: . . . *every American . . . should have the chance to get a good education, to work at a good job with good wages, to raise and provide for a family, to live in safe surroundings, and to retire with dignity and security . . . quality and affordable healthcare is a basic right.*

Clearly the parties chose different approaches, one stressing values and the other policy initiatives. However, both parties agreed in consistently describing America in glowing terms such as: a great nation, a people that prizes candor and fairness, a land of prosperity and liberty.

I recall the story of a little boy on a Pullman train who said to his father as they turned in for the night, "Leave the light on, "I'm afraid to sleep in the dark." The father replied, "You always sleep in the dark at home." And the little boy said, "I know, but that's our dark."

I think as a nation we need to take a long hard look at our own dark. In my mind, America is a seriously sick society, which is not to say every American is sick or that any country not named America is healthy. For me, a working definition of a sick society is one that at any given moment has millions of people:

- Living in conditions of poverty or close to it;
- Out of work;
- Working but not earning anything close to a decent wage;
- Working but definitely not enjoying it;
- Hopelessly in debt;
- Unhappily married;
- Unhappy because they're not married;
- Suffering from depression and anxiety;
- Taking copious quantities of often unnecessary prescription drugs or self-medicating their pain with "illegal" drugs, alcohol and junk food;

- In jail, on their way to jail, spending years in jail and, once out, often going back in;
- Scarred by the effects of racism, sexism and homophobia.

When you then add in our annual rate of murders, suicides, rapes, robberies, arsons, drunk driving, wife beating, child abuse, and white collar crime (or as Woody Guthrie wrote in the song "Pretty Boy Floyd the Outlaw"—some folks will rob you with a six gun and some with a fountain pen) I fail to see how we qualify as a happy and prosperous land of liberty.

In *On Death and Dying* (1969), Elizabeth Kubler-Ross introduced the concept of five stages of grief: denial, anger, bargaining, depression, and acceptance. Her concept has since been expanded to cover events other than grieving for the loss of a loved one. I would apply three of her categories as follows:

Denial: America is in denial when it comes to the large numbers of our fellow countrymen and women, that enjoy neither happiness nor prosperity.

Anger: Most of our anger is directed at the messengers who point out the inability of our society to create a happy and healthy country and not at the system responsible for that failure.

Acceptance: The first step to recovery, in this case, to build systems that enable people to lead happier and more fulfilling lives.

To quote myself from the introduction, "In a healthy society hardly anything is sick and in a sick society hardly anything is healthy." Unless and until we move as a society from sickness to wellness, I am quite certain that the solutions being offered by politicians and pundits of all stripes to the problems currently facing us will prove to be exercises in futility.

The Myth of an Egalitarian and Class-Free Society

Let me start with three events early in our county's history that encapsulate the essence of our class divisions, racial divisions and propensity for violence.

- Bacon's Rebellion.
- The Virginia slave codes.
- Shays's Rebellion.

Bacon's Rebellion took place in colonial Virginia in 1676. High taxes, low prices for tobacco, and resentment against special privileges given those close to the governor provided the background for the uprising. But there was another aspect to the rebellion, namely an assault on Native Americans. Bacon wanted to kill or drive out every Indian in Virginia. In Bacon's own words: "We must defend ourselves against all Indians in general, for that they were all Enemies." The governor of Virginia wouldn't give Bacon a commission to raise an army to drive out the Indians. The governor's refusal to commission Bacon was not based on any desire to live in peace with the Indians; he just didn't want to risk going to war with "friendly" tribes. Bacon then raised his own army and led his followers to a fort held by a friendly tribe. He convinced them to capture warriors from an unfriendly tribe. Bacon's men killed the captives and then promptly turned on their "allies," opening fire on them as well. This kind of betrayal foreshadowed the subsequent acts of aggression against Indian peoples, from forcible expulsion of the Cherokees in the 1830s from their lands in the southeastern United States and their removal to what is now Oklahoma, to the wars against the Indian nations in the West from 1865 to 1890. These actions were not momentary aberrations but had their origins in the very beginnings of our country. It is worth noting that the Cherokees' expulsion was motivated largely by the discovery of gold on their land; in a similar vein the wars against the Indians in the West were largely to open up territories for white settlers. There is yet another aspect to this story. Bacon's followers were both white and black, and the ruling classes of the day feared that this unity might carry over to threaten their economic interests. While Bacon's Rebellion was probably not the direct cause of the Virginia Slave Codes, enacted in 1705, it very likely was a contributing factor. During the latter part of the 17th century, the status of blacks in Virginia had been gradually changing. The black indentured servant was increasingly being replaced by the black slave. In 1705, the Virginia General Assembly defined who was a slave and what status the slave was assigned:

> All servants imported and brought into the Country . . . who were not Christians in their native Country . . . shall be accounted and be slaves. All Negro, mulatto and Indian

slaves within this dominion . . . shall be held to
be real estate. If any slave resist his master . . .
correcting such slave, and shall happen to be
killed in such correction . . . the master shall be
free of all punishment . . . as if such accident
never happened.

The code, which would serve as a model for other
colonies, also included among its provisions that:

- Slaves had to have written permission to leave their
  plantations.
- For robbing or any other major offense, the slave
  would receive 60 lashes and be put in the stocks,
  where his ears would be cut off.
- For an offense such as associating with whites, a
  slave was to be whipped, branded, or maimed.

Shays's rebellion, in Massachusetts in 1786, is an early
example of class struggle and violence. It was precipitated
by several factors: financial difficulties brought about by
a post-revolutionary war economic depression, a credit
squeeze caused by a lack of hard currency, and fiscally
harsh government policies instituted to solve the state's debt
problems. The uprising was put down by force.

Class struggle actually pre-dated the above three events,
going all the way back to the arrival of indentured servants
in the early 1600's. There are contemporary accounts of the
indentured servants running away, protesting their poor

treatment by refusing to work, or appealing to the courts. By the time of the Revolutionary era shoemakers, bakers, printers, and other artisans often struck for higher wages or shorter hours. The common thread running through all those events was employer greed and worker resistance to low wages, long hours, and miserable working conditions.

Starting after the Civil War, America entered into a period of rapid industrialization lasting through WWI and well into the 1930s. Huge corporations, each employing thousands of people, arose in the steel, coal mining, auto, rubber, electrical, trucking, shipping, and other industries. In response, workers formed national unions to protect their interests. Strikes were not only prevalent in those industries but often violent. The records indicate that well over seven hundred workers were killed during those years. The common thread that ran through those strikes was identical to the struggles of working people going back to the 1600's: employer greed and worker resistance.

Since amnesia seems to be built into the human DNA, I would point out that the pattern continues to this day. In 1981 the air traffic controllers went on strike for higher wages, a shorter work week, and better retirement benefits. The strike was broken and I believe set in motion a chain of events that continues today where we are seeing strikes by nurses, teachers and government workers, among others, for decent wages, adequate staffing and preservation of the retirement benefits they have earned and are threatened with losing. And as I write this in November 2012, we are seeing workers in Walmart, one of the most anti-union corporations in America, beginning to resist low wages and the polar opposite of long hours; part-time work without decent sick-leave, health or retirement benefits. Calling the workers "associates" does not disguise the fact that the Walton family, which owns Walmart, is worth some one hundred billion dollars while more than a few of the "associates" are on Medicaid and food stamps. Again, the common thread running through all these strikes is the same common thread going back to the 1600's: capitalism's insatiable drive for profit and worker resistance. In short, we always were, and are today, a class-based society and how anyone can argue that we are a class-free and egalitarian society is beyond me. Again, to use Kubler-Ross's categories:

<u>Denial</u>: America is in denial when it comes to its history of exploitation of workers.

<u>Anger</u>: Most of the anger at this situation is directed at the messengers who point it out and not at the system that fosters it.

<u>Acceptance</u>: The first step to recovery, in this case, to build an economically more just society.

THE MYTH OF A PEACE-LOVING NATION
AND A PEACEABLE PEOPLE

On the Internet I counted 24 wars in which we have been involved, not including our wars with the Indians, which I couldn't find all in one place but with the wars against the Seminoles, Cherokees, Creeks, Comanches, Apaches, Sioux, Nez Perce, and just about every tribe we ever came in contact with, I think 24 wars grossly understates our proclivity for aggression.

I also didn't include our wars in South America. Starting in 1856, we have either gone to war against, sent troops to, skirmished with, meddled with, and covertly (or not so covertly) overthrown the following governments: Costa Rica, Mexico, Ecuador, Brazil, Chile, Uruguay, Grenada, Guyana, Nicaragua, Cuba, Panama, the Dominican Republic, Venezuela, Honduras, Haiti, El Salvador, and I wouldn't be surprised to find that this list is incomplete. In most cases, we didn't go into those countries just once, but over and over. The reasons for these "interventions" ranged from protecting American business interests to, in recent times, fighting communism.

As for the interventions in Central America and the Caribbean, I can do no better than cite General Smedley Butler, who before his death in 1940, was the most highly decorated Marine in U.S. history. After having fought in the Philippines, China, World War 1, and then the Banana Wars (as they were known) in the 1920s and 1930s in Central America and the Caribbean, he said, "I spent 33 years in the Marines, most of my time being a high-class muscle man for Big Business, for Wall Street and the bankers. In short, I was a racketeer for Capitalism."

As for the 24 wars I counted, except for the Revolutionary War, which was a war of liberation from tyranny, and World War II, in which we were attacked and acted in self-defense, all the others were wars of choice. Some of the better known are:

1812: We attacked the British by invading Ontario and Quebec.

1846: We attacked Mexico and, I would note, wound up with one-third of its territory.

1861: The Civil War. Actually only the South, which started the war, was technically the aggressor, but to my point that we are not a peaceable people, it was one of the bloodiest wars in history.

1898: The Spanish-American War.

1917: Our entry into World War 1.

1950: The Korean War.

1960: The Vietnam War.

1991: The Persian Gulf War

2001: The invasion of Iraq.

2003: The invasion of Afghanistan.

Let me make a few observations about our decision to invade Afghanistan in response to the 9/11 al-Qaeda attack on the World Trade Center, the Pentagon, and the attempt to destroy the Capitol; an attempt thwarted, thanks to the heroic action of the passengers.

Given the history of foreign invaders in that country, you would think we might have thought twice and considered other alternatives before we decided that war was the best response. In 1978 there had been a coup in Afghanistan that established an essentially communist government which instituted land reform, women's rights, educational reform and aimed to end feudalism. And it was precisely opposition to land reform, women's rights, educational reform and an end to feudalism that motivated the conservative elements in the country to resist the communist government. The Taliban we are now fighting are essentially the same conservative forces (then the Mujahedin) we supported in their resistance to the Soviet Union, which had sent in troops to support the Afghan communist government. Why we would think we would have any better results than the Soviet Union, which gave up after ten fruitless years of what was their own Vietnam, or England, which also failed in Afghanistan way back in 1839, is beyond me. I don't wish to minimize the complexity of the issues that precipitated our wars in Korea, Vietnam, Iraq or Afghanistan but, again, the fact that we almost always chose war as our response would seem to belie our self-image as a peace-loving nation and a peaceable people.

On a somewhat less global scale, I would note that our proclivity for violence includes the assassination of four presidents: Lincoln, Garfield, McKinley, and Kennedy, not to mention a few that were shot but not killed. And the list would not be complete without adding Martin Luther King, Jr.; Malcolm X; Medgar Evers; Viola Luizzo; Michael Schwerner, James Chaney and Andrew Goodman; the four young girls in a Birmingham church; and the countless others killed in the civil rights struggles. And even that list would not be complete without noting our violence towards abortion providers, gays, lesbians, bisexuals, and transgendered people, as well as the constant inner city violence and consistently occurring mass murders throughout the country.

Let me end by noting that human violence long preceded capitalism and I do not think that indigenous peoples were necessarily paragons of virtue or living in an earthly paradise. From everything I have read, they did quite well when it came to rape, murder and wars, without any help from the Europeans. As for our own aggressive behaviors, painful as they are to acknowledge, they pale into insignificance when compared to the atrocities committed during the 1930s and 1940s by Hitler's Nazi Germany, Stalin's Soviet Union, and Hirohito's Imperial Japan. I would also note that the greed and cruelty of the European colonial empires in Africa, Asia and South America far exceeded in scope and brutality our own imperialistic forays. However, I've never been impressed with the argument that "The other guy is worse." I will once more use Kubler-Ross's categories:

<u>Denial</u>: America is in denial when it comes to our history of wars and aggression toward others and our own internal violence.

<u>Anger</u>: Again, most of the anger is directed at the messengers who point this out and not at the system that fosters the violence.

<u>Acceptance</u>: The first step to recovery, in this case, building a less violent society.

PART 2

A Contrarian View on Five of the Many Major Problems America faces: Crime, Racism, Foreign Policy, Trade and Immigration.

CRIME

Both the Republicans and Democrats are opposed to crime and want justice for the victims. If platitudes could eliminate criminal behavior, we would be crime-free tomorrow morning. The Republicans are more likely than the Democrats to stress punishment, longer jail sentences, the right to bear arms, reliance on strong families, and faith-based programs. What drives me to distraction are sentences like these from the Republican platform:

On gambling: *Millions of Americans suffer from the problem of pathological gambling that can destroy families. We support the law prohibiting gambling over the Internet.*

I find it fascinating that the party of less government interference into the lives of people proposes to prohibit Internet gambling. What I find even more fascinating is that nothing is said about lotteries, horse racing, and sports betting. I remember when the numbers, horse racing, and sports betting were the exclusive province of your favorite numbers runner or bookie. I can still recall the lurid headlines of those days about the "poor wives and children" that suffered because of a husband's gambling. I remember the regular raids on bookie joints, with people being sent to jail—except for those who bribed the police, district attorneys, or judges. While I'm fussing at the Republicans, I should note that liberal Democrats—support as much if not more so than Republicans—probably not only lotteries but any gambling they can tax.

On prison reform the Republicans state: *Public authorities at all levels must cooperate to regain control of the nation's correctional institutions. It is unacceptable that prison officers should live in fear of the inmates they guard.*

I am quite sure that more than a few prisoners are violent or are sociopaths, and otherwise disagreeable to be around. However, I am convinced that only the Republicans could think that the major prison reform needed is to protect the officers from the inmates, a thought that strikes me as somewhere between bizarre and paranoid.

On children: *Breaking the cycle of crime begins with the children of those who are incarcerated. Deprived of a parent through no fault of their own, these youngsters should be a special concern of our schools, social services, and religious institutions. Government at all levels should work with faith-based institutions that have proven track records in diverting young and first offenders from criminal careers through Second Chance and similar programs . . . given the weight of social science evidence concerning the crucial role played by the traditional family in setting a child's future course, we urge a thoughtful review of governmental policies and programs to ensure that they do not undermine that institution.*

Not a word about the parents separated from their children by excessively harsh sentences for "crimes" such as drug use and prostitution. Not a word about their continued victimization after release through policies that make finding work problematic for many. Not a word about low-wage jobs that force many single mothers, married mothers, fathers and husbands, to work two jobs and still be unable to provide their children with the benefits of the "traditional" family. Not a word about their constant efforts to cut funds for everything from Head-Start to after-school programs, which actually do help support the traditional family.

As for the Democrats, when it comes to crime, they say much the same thing: *As Democrats, we are committed to being smart on crime . . . . that means being tough on violent crime . . . . and holding offenders accountable.* But somehow or other it seems to me that their heart really isn't in it. When you read the totality of their platform it is clear they would much prefer to correct the social ills they feel are the root cause of crime, so I am inclined to give them a pass.

Way back in the 1960s, I was harangued by one of my radical friends to the effect that crime is a political statement more than a criminal act. At the time I was working my way through college driving a cab and I was mugged four times during my cab-driving stint, so I wasn't particularly sympathetic to criminals. Despite that, my response was, "Yes, it is a political statement. The question is whether it is a good-bad and/or effective-ineffective statement." Since the discussion focused on "street" crime, I pointed out that as a general rule the person being robbed/mugged/assaulted tended to blame the perpetrator rather than the system. As a result, the expression then current—"A conservative is a liberal who has been mugged"—had a great deal of validity, making the task of those wanting to change society for the better that much more difficult. Also, since most of those making those "political" statements usually wound up in jail, hardly ever made a decent living from their "political" activities, and quite often wound up dead at an early age, I didn't think that mugging, robbing, assaulting and drug dealing were great career choices. Nor did it strike me as a particularly useful way to express one's displeasure with our social system.

In the interest of full disclosure, let me say that if someone murdered a family member or one of my friends, as a general rule I would like to see the perpetrator shot—immediately. In fact, I would like to carry it out personally. I would like them tied to a stake (no blindfold) so that I could shoot them slowly, starting at the feet, moving up to the ankles, the thighs, the groin, moving over to the wrists, the elbows, the shoulders, carefully avoiding all vital organs and only then reluctantly putting them out of their misery with a well-placed bullet to the head or heart. However, having said that, I can do no better than recall former New York State Governor Mario Cuomo's comment that personally he was in favor of the death penalty but would like to live in a society that protected him from his own worst impulses. Clearly I need a lot of protection from my own worst impulses but I suspect I am not alone in that regard—all the more reason for trying to create a utopian society.

So, with that rant out of the way, I propose that once we have established a society in which there is full employment at a living wage, and our need for food, shelter and clothing has been met, we redefine criminal activity as follows: Any behavior that preys on another human being, for whatever reason, shall be considered criminal.

As a start I think we should define capitalism as a criminal enterprise since it definitely preys on people. Paying people a fraction of the value of the wealth they produce through their hard work so that *you* live well and they *don't* strikes me as criminal. Manipulating financial markets; speculating; driving up commodity prices; persuading people (and governments) to take out risky loans with over-blown promises; writing tax laws to permit the wealthy to escape paying taxes, thus forcing the rest of us to pay more—all strike me as falling under the definition of "preying" on people and therefore criminal.

I would be remiss if I didn't note the striking parallels between drug pushers and those corporations that pushed cigarettes (when they were allowed to) and those currently pushing alcohol and junk food. I don't particularly object to alcohol but I do object to the way it is marketed. No matter the cost to society, in their pursuit of profits both the drug pushers and the corporations are constantly "pushing" people to consume ever more quantities of the products they are selling, products that are certainly dangerous when used in excess. I have difficulty calling the drug pushers "criminals" and the corporate CEO's pushing junk food and alcohol "respectable" businessmen.

The irony of our current efforts to control crime is that capitalism needs crime It particularly needs street crime, ranging from mugging to armed robbery to murder; it provides capitalism with scapegoats, a diversion, a way to divide people. Crime has become the basis for a capitalist industry that provides employment for many and, with the privatization of prisons, yields huge corporate profits.

Utopia, unlike capitalism, will not need crime and can come to the table with clean hands. Since utopia will offer everyone the chance to work and receive a living wage, it is in a position to occupy the moral high ground when it comes to combating crime: it can be tough on crime while simultaneously providing meaningful rehabilitation for those who have committed crimes.

As for drugs, once we rid ourselves of the war on drugs, a "war" that didn't work with alcohol back in the days of prohibition and isn't working now with drugs, we can treat drug addiction without criminalizing it. We can break the back of the drug-dealing cartels overnight. All we need to do is dispense drugs free at clinics while encouraging the users to enter treatment. If the users can "do" drugs and function, that is, work and not engage in anti-social behaviors such as mugging, burglary, armed robbery and murder, so be it. However, if they can't function, are a public nuisance, and their family and friends can't keep them from harming others, utopia, occupying as it does the moral high ground, will have the necessary political consensus to confine them to rehab (not jail) as often as necessary. If utopia comes too late for them, we'll just have to accept the responsibility of treating them humanely for their lifetime as one of those burdens we have inherited.

I'm pessimistic that utopia can eliminate all the criminal behaviors that so bedevil us currently, but I'm optimistic that it can significantly reduce the number of such behaviors.

Racism

Following are some excerpts from the Republican Party statement on equal rights. *Individual rights and the responsibilities that go with them are the foundation of a free society . . . . our commitment to equal opportunity extends from landmark school-choice legislation for the students of Washington D.C. to historic appointments at the highest levels of government.*

And I always thought the landmark decision was Brown v. Wade declaring separate but equal unconstitutional, not the choice to go to charter schools.

The statement goes on: *As a matter of principle, Republicans oppose any attempts to create race-based governments within the United States, as well as any domestic governments not bound by the Constitution or the Bill of Rights.*

For the life of me I can't figure out what they are talking about. I think what they are saying is that they are not only opposed to any form of affirmative action on the federal and state levels but, just in case any city or municipality is thinking of attempting to do something to redress the effects of racism (which in their minds is to create a "race based" government), they can forget about it.

There's more: *Precisely because we oppose discrimination, we reject preferences, quotas, and set-asides, whether in education or in corporate boardrooms. The government should not make contracts on this basis, and neither should corporations.* Only in America could the party of less government interference in the lives of the people decide in the same sentence that not only the government but also corporations should be prevented from entering into contracts of their choice.

I really don't like to pick on the Democrats because at least their hearts are in the right place, but, as usual, by the time you have finished reading their section on equal rights your eyes will have glazed over from the sheer verbiage. Although they start off simply enough by affirming their belief in equal rights for all, it isn't long before they have wandered off into *We will restore professionalism in the Department of Justice . . . reaffirm our support for the Equal Rights Amendment . . . pursue a foreign and domestic policy that promotes civil and human rights . . . support the White House Initiative on Asian-American and Pacific Islanders . . . including enforcement on disaggregation of Census data.*

I know full well what that last statement means, but it is truly deserving of some kind of award, for why stop when you are on a roll? And they don't stop, they just go on-and-on. I don't know who wrote the Democratic Party platform, but I'm certain they must have been charging by the word.

Back in the early 1900's, W.E.B. Dubois said race would be the defining issue of the twentieth century in America. As much as I admire the writings of DuBois, I think he was off by some 300 years. I would say race has been the defining issue in America at least since Virginia enacted the slave codes in 1705 and has continued through the establishment of Jim Crow laws in the post-Civil War South, the de facto segregation in the North, the constant attempts to roll back the gains of the civil rights movement and a judicial system that to this day disproportionately jails blacks.

There is no way you can reduce people to chattel and segregate and exclude them without developing an all-encompassing racist ideology to justify the awfulness of what you are doing. Even the term "race" is misleading. One of the definitions of a species is that it is capable of inter-breeding and producing fertile offspring. Since human beings have been cheerfully (and sometimes not so cheerfully, as when rape has been the by-product of conquest) producing fertile offspring whenever they have come in contact with one another, we are clearly one species and not four or five races. Race, however, is so pervasive in our society that we are always aware of it and yet, for whites, practically unconscious of its myriad manifestations. There is an unbelievably long history of racist writings all aimed at rationalizing and justifying America's long and sorry racist history. There is also a rich and voluminous history of excellent writings on race in America, so I will limit my contribution to the following anecdotes.

Well over 30 years ago I was doing a workshop on multiculturalism with a black female colleague. Since the emphasis was on communication and perceptions, we asked the program host to introduce us only by name and residence, to instruct the audience to complete the small written quiz in the front of the workbook, and to explain that we would introduce ourselves. The quiz asked them to circle the answer that best described each of us.

<u>Religion</u>: *Jewish, Catholic, Protestant.* The group took one look at me and 90% said Jewish. A few figured Moscou was a French or, perhaps Rumanian, name and checked off Catholic. Everybody checked off Protestant for my colleague. She was Catholic, as were her parents, grandparents, great-grandparents all the way back for hundreds of years.

<u>Marital status</u>: *Single, Married, Divorced.* Most thought we both were married but she got more unmarried citations.

<u>Residence</u>: *Apartment Renter, Home Owner.* Since I had been introduced as a New Yorker, there was some logic in assuming, as many did, that I was an apartment renter. Those who made that selection for me almost always picked apartment renter for my colleague as well even though she had been introduced as living in New Jersey, where home ownership was a likely choice. She was a home-owner.

<u>Income level</u>: *$50,000-$75,000, $75,000-$100,000, $100,000-$200,000.* Whatever they chose for me also represented the upper limit of what they thought she might be earning.

<u>Educational Attainment</u>: *Bachelor of Arts, Bachelor of Science, Master's Degree, PhD, Post-doctoral Studies.* The pattern of previous answers was repeated. I had a Bachelor's

degree and she had a doctorate, yet she was consistently rated, at best, as being only on a par with me.

Before giving the group the correct answers, we briefly introduced ourselves. My colleague said she had never been married and was a single parent with a nine-year-old daughter and a seven-year-old son. You could read the body language in the room like an open book. For the whites the words that come to mind are smugness (Of course. Isn't that just typical of them?) For the blacks, shame, embarrassment and annoyance that she felt it necessary to disclose this. After an appropriately dramatic pause my colleague went on to say: "Two years ago I adopted a seven-year-old girl and although I had only intended to adopt one child, when I found out she had a five-year-old brother who had been placed in a separate foster home, I decided that I had to adopt him as well." Again, the body language would have been funny if it hadn't been so revealing (and sad) of the pervasive negative implications of being black in white America. You could literally see the whites denying to themselves that they had even for a moment drawn any negative conclusions from her earlier remarks and the blacks heaving a sigh of relief.

Perhaps more importantly, race so trumps rational thinking in our society that probably no one took a moment to wonder what kind of foster care system separates a brother and a sister or what kind of social system produces the dysfunction that separates parents from their children.

In the course of the workshop, a young white woman got up and said (and well over 30 years later I can still remember her exact words), "I'm on the Black History Month committee in my company and I'm not the least bit prejudiced but I don't see why we have to have a Black History Month. I mean, we want to get rid of racism and just treat each other as human beings and as a white person I certainly don't see any need for a White History Month." Don't even think of asking me how she wound up on the Black History Month committee.

Since this was before personal computers became all-pervasive, I didn't have today's computer terminology to explain to her that in our society "white" is the default position. Instead, I went into a lengthy explanation that in the absence of identifying a particular accomplishment as black, we assume it is white. I then moved on to the concept of the "other" and pointed out that when a white person commits a crime we whites don't see it as a reflection on whites, but when a black person commits a crime that is exactly how we see it. To drive the point home, I mentioned that Hitler and the Nazis had murdered some six million Jews, untold Gypsies, Russians, Poles, and just about anybody else they could get their hands on, but so far as I knew, no one drew the conclusion that whites are a vicious, barbaric people. At this point I became aware that I was making the young woman distinctly uncomfortable, so I tried my best to soften my comments by moving away from race to gays. I said,—and this was somewhat before the fairly recent advent of gays onto the national stage—"I have no idea how many gay people there are in America, but I would guess that if we could identify them and ban them from the arts, at least half of the music, movies, theater, literature and actors we enjoy would vanish overnight. So, if you think about it from the standpoint of a gay person, not only do we literally steal all of their work but we add insult to injury by not even knowing we stole it."

Just as I was about to make the point that the reason we need a Black History Month is because so much of the contribution of blacks to America is either unknown or discounted, my colleague interjected: "You notice Jack didn't think to mention fashion and design. As a black woman, I felt compelled to come here dressed impeccably while he had the freedom to show up without a jacket or tie, just wearing slacks and a shirt" (which I thought was a low blow, since I was wearing brown shoes, brown socks, brown pants, and a brown shirt, and in my mind was perfectly color-coordinated). It was also the first time, after having done dozens of workshops with her, that I even thought about why she was always impeccably dressed. When I asked her how come she had never mentioned this to me, her response was, "Do you have any idea how exhausting it is to educate white folks about what it means to be black in white America?"

Just in case anyone reacts by saying this took place well over thirty years ago and we've come a long way since then—and I think we have, but nowhere near as far as conservatives fear and liberals would like to believe—I offer the following anecdote. (I'm going to take a very long story and ask you to trust me that I am being faithful to the truth of the situation even while I omit, change, or shorten many of the actual events and weave several different strands into a single composite.)

About five years ago I was approached by an organization to do some consulting.

They: "We think that our younger black and Latino employees are disaffected and we would like to run some focus groups with them to see what the problem may be."

Me (using my best Consulting 101 skills): "You think your younger Black and Latino employees are disaffected so you would like to run some focus groups to see what the problem may be?"

They: "Yes, that's it, exactly."

Me (remembering that I was long since retired and very particular about the assignments I took): "Let me see if I understand you. You think the younger black and Latino employees are disaffected so you want to hire an old white guy to find out what's bothering them?"

They grasped the irony. In fact, I believe they grasped the depth of subconscious racism in their decision-making process, so after we agreed that we would find an African-American or Latino to co-lead with me, I took the assignment.

We ran focus groups with representation from all the staff, not just the younger black and Latino employees. It turned out that the most disaffected employees were the white women! After listening to the black and Latino participants, my conclusion was not that they weren't disaffected but that they simply didn't expect much more from the organization than what they experienced in the rest of America and held the organization to a lower standard than the white women.

Since we love success stories showing our progress on the racial front, I offer this one with the *caveat* that the lesson to be drawn is not how much people of good will can accomplish, but how deeply embedded racism is in the fabric of our society. Most of the black and Latino complaints focused on evaluations they perceived to be overly critical and on not getting the kinds of assignments that would prepare them for promotions. One young black woman in the group had in fact not only been promoted several times but was obviously on a fast career track. As she described her situation, her supervisor (a white female) made sure she got her fair share of the best assignments. This meant she worked with many different groups and managers throughout the organization. Her supervisor mentored her work and progress on all those assignments and when evaluation time came, her supervisor made sure that all the managers with whom the young woman had worked sent in evaluations. Since she was intimately familiar with the quality of the young woman's work, any evaluation that she felt did not accurately represent the quality of young woman's work was sent back with a demand for an explanation.

Actually, this is just plain good management and probably ninety percent of white employees would give their right arm for this kind of supervisor. But arguing that we are not a racist society because we treat our "own" equally badly, or that thanks to the good will of some whites, some blacks make it, or that some blacks overcome all obstacles and make it anyhow, hardly strikes me as a convincing argument that racism is a thing of the past.

Conservatives object to "social engineering" designed to foster integration. I would point out that white (Anglo-Saxon protestant) America has from the very beginning used social engineering to exclude blacks from virtually every aspect of American life. The fact that at one time or another they also excluded just about everybody else who, for whatever reason, was deemed "different" doesn't negate the fact that anti-black racism was, and is, qualitatively different from anti-Semitism, anti-Catholicism, anti-Irish, anti-Slavic, or "anti-" any other group, that by virtue of a white skin sooner or later were accepted into mainstream America.

Exclusion and separation breed fear, resentment, and distrust. We need to find a way for people to live together with shared values as the common denominator or, to reference Martin Luther King, we need to judge people by the content of their character and not by the color of their skin; or by their gender; religion (or lack of it); their sexual preferences; their disabilities or whatever it is that separates "them" from "us".

Far from running away from integration, as conservatives would have us do, we need to actively embrace it in all its myriad forms and develop a conscious ethos of integration as truly American—or should I say utopian? I take you back yet again to Kubler-Ross's categories:

Denial: America is in denial when it comes to the pervasiveness of racism in our society.

Anger: Our anger is directed not at the systemic racism in our society but at the messengers who point it out and the victims themselves.

Acceptance: The first stage in recovery, in this case, realizing that before we can have a post-racial color-blind society we must first confront our long, and sorry, history of racism.

Foreign Policy

Before discussing foreign policy I will simply note without comment that in their respective foreign policy planks the Republicans managed to include opposing abortion and homosexuals in the military and the Democrats managed to include a G.I. Bill of Rights and assistance to veterans facing foreclosure.

Once again, I find myself keeping company with George Washington, who in that same farewell address I quoted earlier warned us to beware of foreign entanglements and avoid overgrown military establishments. Washington saw them as inimical to liberty and advised us to steer clear of permanent alliances with any portion of the foreign world. I would also point out that another military commander who became president, Dwight D. Eisenhower, warned in his farewell address to the presidency some 160 years after Washington:

> In the councils of government, we must guard against the acquisition of unwarranted influence, whether sought or unsought, by the military- industrial complex. The potential for the disastrous rise of misplaced power exists and will persist. We must never let the weight of this combination endanger our liberties or democratic processes. We should take nothing

> for granted. Only an alert and knowledgeable citizenry can compel the proper meshing of the huge industrial and military machinery of defense with our peaceful methods and goals, so that security and liberty may prosper together.

As I write this, I know that 2013 is not the late 18th century, but I think that back in 1796, Washington had it right, and in 1961, Dwight D. Eisenhower also had it right.

As a start, I would propose that we close all our military bases wherever they may be and bring our troops and all their accompanying private contractors home. Far from keeping us safe, our military bases around the world breed resentment and hostility and simply give our enemies more places in which to strike out at us. If anyone does decide to go to war with us, the countries we are "protecting" will probably be among the first to suffer. To add insult to injury, those bases do virtually nothing to improve the quality of life for the overwhelming majority of citizens in those countries while making the improvement of our own quality of life that much more difficult. As to the argument that America is the one indispensable country in the world and our bases keep those countries, and us, free and independent from aggressors, all I can say is that there are probably better ways to accomplish that goal and history teaches that empires inevitably come to a bad end.

Next, we should withdraw from the United Nations. I regard the UN as a failed organization and, at the risk of causing *Why Not Utopia?* to be dismissed as isolationist, nativist, and naïve, I suggest that we leave the UN and build new bilateral agreements with other countries and/or a new international organization. As to the failure of the UN, I quote from Article 1 of its statement of purpose:

> To maintain international peace and security, and to that end to take effective collective measures for the prevention and removal of threats to the peace, and for the suppression of acts of aggression or other breaches of the peace, and to bring about by peaceful means and in conformity with the principles of justice and international law, adjustment or settlement of international disputes or situations which might lead to a breach of the peace.

I researched online for wars since 1945 and found two lists, one from 1945 to 1989 and one from 1990 to 2002 and came up with something like 203 wars. Granted, alongside major wars such as Korea, Vietnam, the Israeli-Arab wars, both Iraq wars, our current war (ongoing as of this writing in February 2013) in Afghanistan, and Russia's past war in Afghanistan, the lists also included various small local insurrections such as The East Prigorodny War: a war that was an inter-ethnic conflict in the eastern part of the Prigorodny District of the Republic of North Ossetia-Alania, which began in 1989 and developed during

1992 into a brief ethnic war between local Ingush and Ossetian paramilitary forces. According to Helsinki Human Rights Watch, the Ossetian militia orchestrated a campaign of ethnic cleansing during October and November of 1992, resulting in the deaths of more than 600 Ingush civilians and the expulsion of approximately 60,000 Ingush from the Prigorodny District. I should note that for the 600 killed and the 60,000 expelled from their homes, listing this as a "small" war does not do justice to the human suffering involved.

However, what clearly emerges from the list is that the United Nations has been spectacularly unsuccessful in achieving its stated purpose of maintaining international peace and security.

Article 2 states:

> All Members shall settle their international disputes by peaceful means in such a manner that international peace and security, and justice, are not endangered. All Members shall refrain in their international relations from the threat or use of force against the territorial integrity or political independence of any state, or in any other manner inconsistent with the Purposes of the United Nations.

I don't buy the argument that without the UN there would have been even more wars and/or the wars that did take place would have been even bloodier and longer lasting. Since I can't prove a negative, I will simply repeat my earlier comment and say that even if that argument were true, the record is so awful that the organization should be disbanded and some attempt to start over be initiated.

Article 4 states:

> Membership in the United Nations is open to all other peace- loving states which accept the obligations contained in the present Charter and, in the judgment of the Organization, are able and willing to carry out these obligations.

Clearly, if the UN believed what it says, given our track record—and I hasten to include Russia, England, France, China, most of the countries of Africa and the Mid-East—never mind *our* leaving the UN, the UN should be kicking us and just about everybody else out. The list of nations *not* currently, or in the recent past, in default of the UN charter is depressingly small.

Once we leave the UN we could try to develop bilateral relationships wherever feasible. We could approach every country and say *mea culpa* (even if no *mea culpa* is warranted) and say we would like to live in peace with them and start over. If we "like" their social and political system and are comfortable with their cultural ethos (and they with ours), and we both agree to renounce war except in self-defense, we could consider establishing guidelines detailing the extent of our relationship. If we are uncomfortable, ranging from mild discomfort to truly despising everything they stand for, we can consider keeping relations to as minimal a level as self-interest dictates or (self-interest or not) having nothing—and I mean nothing—to do with them. No trade, no diplomatic relations, no travel. Nothing.

I am definitely not suggesting a "Stop the world I want to get off!" policy nor am I suggesting unilateral disarmament. From 9/11, to free-lance terrorists, to North Korea and Iran, to possible threats arising from unexpected places, the world is a scary place. However, having said that, I think the concept of "fortress America" makes sense, and given our military might, I think most—if not all—potential enemies will come to the conclusion that any attack on us would end much more badly for them than for us.

As to fears that this would leave innocent people to the not-so-tender mercies of the despots and tyrants who currently rule them; subject women to continued oppression from patriarchal societies, or leave weaker countries at the mercy of stronger and ill-intentioned neighbors, all I can say is that I think our current policies have proven as useless in that regard as have those of the UN. In fact, I think *not* meddling in the affairs of other countries but setting an example by the way we live is more likely to bring about change for the better in those countries than our current policies do. As to the argument that the UN has done invaluable humanitarian work throughout the world, there is nothing I am suggesting that would prevent us or any other country—or the UN, even if we're not in it—from doing invaluable humanitarian work throughout the world.

And last, but certainly not least, I find our government's policy of hiring people to die for us via a volunteer army totally immoral. I am certain the government does this because it knows full well that if we each have to risk dying it will be unable to whip up sentiment for *any* war that is not truly a war of self-defense. Therefore, I propose that in all future wars we draft everybody—young and old, male and female, the healthy and the not so healthy—so that we all have to put our lives on hold, sacrifice equally, and equally risk being killed, wounded or possibly maimed for life.

FREE TRADE

In all probability trade has been part of the human existence from our first appearance on earth. When that trade was confined to small human bands living relatively close by and was based primarily on a barter system, it probably was free. I wouldn't be the least bit surprised, though, to find out that each group tried to get the best deal for itself even if it meant cheating the other group. I don't think anything like *free* trade has existed for a long time. Once nation states and powerful corporations arose it seems that the predominant pattern has been to take what you want by force. Everything from the slave trade to occupying the lands of others and ripping off their natural wealth, to destroying their local economies, makes a mockery of the belief that trade, especially under capitalism, is, or can be, free. Since trade today consistently follows the path of cheap labor, powerful corporations and countries are able to rig the system, making free trade a mockery for the less powerful.

Nevertheless, both the Republican and Democratic Party platforms are firmly in favor of free trade. Some typical comments on free trade from both party platforms are:

- Given a level playing field America can out-compete anybody.
- An aggressive trade strategy is especially important with regard to agriculture.

- We must also show leadership at the World Trade Organization.
- We need tougher negotiators on our side of the table.
- Almost a decade into this century, we still have no coherent strategy to compete in a global economy.

What I find most striking is the use of words like "aggressive" and "tougher" and the highly problematic assertion that given a level playing field we can out-compete everybody. The fact is that at present, many countries are out-competing us in everything from manufacturing, literacy, education, science and math, to quality of life.

The Republican platform specifically says: *An aggressive trade strategy is especially important with regard to agriculture. Our farm economy produces for the world; its prosperity depends, more than ever before, on open markets. U.S. agricultural exports will top $100 billion this year. We will contest any restrictions upon our farm products within the World Trade Organization and will work to make the WTO's decision-making process more receptive to the arguments of American producers.*

As for pursuing an aggressive agricultural policy to export our foods to other countries, I fail to see the logic of producing food here and shipping it thousands of miles away to countries that, absent Western distortions of their economy, would be able to produce their own food. To speak of opening up their markets to our agricultural products in the name of free trade is to disguise the fact that we have consigned whole countries to agricultural serfdom by taking up their arable land to produce not food for themselves but single-crop farm products for export to us and other first-world countries. We are not talking free trade; we are talking economic exploitation. That being said, free trade is an oxymoron that serves only to leave corporations "free" to beggar everybody in their rush for maximum profits.

As for getting tougher negotiators on our side of the table, what happens if they simply put tougher negotiators on their side of the table? I guess the assumption is if we can out-compete everybody we can also out-negotiate them. To those who nevertheless insist we can out-compete everybody if only we had a level playing field, I would pose the following question: if, on a level playing field, we really can out-compete the rest of the world, why would the rest of the world want to trade with us? Clearly there is no point in playing if you are bound to lose. All you have to do is look at our own hand-wringing over the trade deficits we keep running up with countries like China and Japan to realize that losing results in a constant search to change the playing field in order to move from loser to winner. A utopian approach would be to stop trying to out-compete everybody and instead start trying to develop win-win solutions.

IMMIGRATION

Republicans and Democrats both agree that we need comprehensive reform of our immigration policy. Whether that means building barbed wire electrified fences to keep "illegal aliens" out, or providing a pathway to citizenship for those already here, or something in-between, depends on whether one is a conservative, liberal, or something in-between. As I write this (February 2013), Congress is debating a comprehensive immigration reform bill. At the risk of being seen as cynical I am certain that the bill, if they even manage to come up with one, will not be comprehensive and will certainly not solve the problem, which is that we need to keep "importing" people because we need their cheap labor. So I herewith offer a distinctly contrarian view.

Immigration was undoubtedly a good thing from the time the first Europeans arrived until at least the 20th century, if by a "good thing" you mean it helped build the country we now live in. Of course, if you happened to be a Native American it was definitely not a good thing. I wasn't around back then to talk to native peoples, but somehow I think that what we called immigration they called invasion (correctly, to my mind) and what we called settling the country they called stealing their land (also correctly, to my mind.) The number of Native Americans actually killed by force may not have risen to the level of genocide although if you include those killed by coming in contact with Western diseases and starvation resulting from our policies it well may have. If nothing else, the fact that we settled native peoples on reservations, deliberately removed children from their parents and sent them away to schools to learn "civilized" ways and forbade them to use their native languages and religious traditions certainly qualifies as cultural genocide. So my contrarian thought is, never mind deporting all the "illegal aliens" (read: Mexicans and Latin Americans); let's do the right thing by the original inhabitants and all go back to where *we* came from.

When it comes to immigration, there is an unbroken line from today's conservatives, out to deport "illegal aliens," all the way back to 1816, when the American Colonization Society was founded to resettle free blacks in Africa. In 1855, the "Know-Nothing" Party, officially named the American Party—with roots going back to anti-immigrant fervor of the 1830s—was established with the aim of keeping the Irish out of the country. In the late 19th century and continuing well into the 1940s, attempts to keep out Asians, Jews, Italians, Eastern Europeans and virtually everyone not of Northern European descent were an ongoing part of our political scene.

Immigration at the present time cannot be pigeon-holed into one-size-fits-all policy. It seems to me there are two significant immigrant groups: unskilled and largely undocumented workers and those with scientific and technical skills. In the case of the former, whom conservatives insist on seeing as taking American jobs, taking advantage of our welfare system, causing us to spend our precious dollars to provide for their health care and education for their children, my solution is simple: whether the number is six million, ten million, twelve million or twenty million, round them all up and deport them immediately. Overnight. No exceptions. I figure as soon as we realize that we would then have to do our own work, it would take no more than two weeks before the entire country would be down on its hands and knees begging the unskilled, undocumented workers to come back and offering to double their wages.

Once they agreed to come back, we could make the farm workers among them supervisors and foremen, teaching the rest of us how to plant, weed, pick crops, work on ranches, and do all the other things we need to learn so that "we can earn our daily bread by the sweat of our brow," which seems far more honorable to me than making other people do the work for us. In return for the above services, we could grant them the normal path to citizenship: apply, wait five years and pass a test. The only flaw I see in this theory is that other countries might decide to sue us for stealing their best, most ambitious, and hardest-working people. (Even as, in the world of sports if you try to entice away another team's player you get fined for tampering.)

Since I object in principle to exploiting others, I would like to extend this solution to all the other occupations: construction, hotel service, restaurant work, car washes, landscaping, child care—wherever we seem to think nothing of getting immigrants to work for us and then add insult to injury by paying them a pittance of the value they produce. As with undocumented farm workers turned supervisors and foremen, we could do the same with all the other occupations. The thought that a chambermaid from Mexico, Guatemala or elsewhere in Latin America, forced by economic circumstances to leave her family—often including her children—would become a supervisor teaching middle-class Americans how to make beds and clean toilets is enough to make me want to go out and book a hotel room whether I need one or not. And since I also object to gender-assigned roles, I see no reason why men shouldn't be chambermaids. In fact, if the aforementioned women were to train men—I'm thinking politicians, bankers, stockbrokers, pundits, for starters—to do the work, forget about a room, I'll book a suite.

The second group, one that doesn't seem to worry us as much, consists of skilled workers in the technical and scientific fields. Since we have a shortage of people in those areas and our corporations need them as workers and our universities need them as graduate students, not only do we welcome them but we encourage them *not* to go back home. I am well aware that many of the skilled and scientific workers coming here from the underdeveloped countries *want* to be here. However, they represent the flip side of "guest" workers. First the empire preys on the misery it has created in colonized countries to provide itself with a steady stream of cheap labor. Then the empire avails itself of the best and brightest from those countries, draining the colonized countries of the educated and highly skilled human capital they desperately need to become modern democratic, industrial states.

In short, it is my contrarian opinion that our comprehensive immigration policy should be:

- Set a five-year moratorium on immigration with the exception of those already in the pipeline;
- Offer citizenship to everyone currently here, complete with family reunification;
- Develop a five-year plan to determine how many people our land can sustain;
- Develop a rational (win-win) immigration policy in consultation with those countries that have a significant stake in our immigration policies.

PART 3

**Utopian planning and
Capitalist Free Enterprise**

Utopia and Capitalism

It has long been noted that war is too important to be left to the generals. I would add that the economy is too important to be left to the vagaries of the free enterprise market system, particularly because those vagaries always seem to entail a great deal of economic inequality and insecurity. *Why Not Utopia?* will propose a dual social and economic system: utopian socialist planning co-existing with capitalistic free enterprise. However, I would stress this will be a utopian government, and utopia and capitalism will not be equal partners; capitalism will definitely be the junior partner.

A necessary first step toward building a co-existing utopian socialist society and capitalist free-enterprise system is to distinguish between public and private goods and services and societal and individual interests. As a start, and I stress just as a start, to get the conversation going, I would list the following as falling under the rubric of public goods: food, shelter and clothing; under societal interests: health care, education and national defense. Simply stated, this means that if people want to guarantee themselves the public goods and services listed above they will have to plan and work co-operatively to achieve those goals.

I would define private goods and services as anything that people want that utopia can't or won't or fails to provide, such as alcohol; sugary foods and beverages; fur coats, jewelry, luxury yachts, houses with 20,000 square feet of space; "subversive" culture, that is any culture that does not uphold utopian ideals. If utopia is to be a free society and avoid becoming either a nanny state or a dictatorship, the free-enterprise system must be allowed to step in and provide those goods and services. To borrow from Abraham Maslow's hierarchy of needs, utopia must allow people the freedom to pursue their need for self-actualization.

THE BASIC FOUNDATION OF UTOPIA

The Republican 2008 convention platform can be summarized as follows: *America's free economy has given our country the world's highest standard of living, allows us to share our prosperity with the rest of humanity, is an engine of charity empowering everything from the Sabbath collection plate to great endowments, creates opportunity, rewards self-reliance and hard work, and unleashes productive energies that other societies can only imagine . . .*

I don't think I am being unfair when I say that virtually every solution the Republicans offer to improve the economy or create jobs starts with cutting taxes and ends with reducing regulations.

By way of contrast, the Democratic Party offers a wonderfully feel-good wish-list of platitudes:

- Good jobs with good pay and benefits;
- Strengthen the right of workers to organize into unions;
- Improve workplace safety;
- Raise the minimum wage;
- Expand family and medical leave;
- Provide flexible work arrangements;
- Expand the childcare tax credit;
- Provide every child access to quality, affordable early childhood education;

- Double the funding for after school and summer learning opportunities for children;
- Provide assistance to those working men and women of this country who do the heroic job of providing care for their aging relatives.

And that's not even the whole list! No decent liberal would quarrel with any of those sentiments; but if anyone believes the Democrats, or capitalism, are capable of accomplishing those goals I have a bridge I want to sell you.

I suggest that in utopia we use the KISS (Keep It Simple, Stupid) approach. Guarantee everyone full employment at a living wage—one that enables you to purchase all the food you need, a really decent place to live, enough clothing for all seasons and all occasions; also provide for all the health care and education both needed and wanted; and allow enough leisure time to enjoy life.

You work and you live well. You don't work and you've got a problem, or your family or friends have a problem if they let you sponge off them.

WORK IN UTOPIA

First and foremost, we need to become a society that does our own work. We need to stop exploiting workers, whether our own workers, "guest" workers, "undocumented" workers or workers in other countries. When you can make more money as a politician, banker, lawyer, athlete, consultant, stockbroker, TV reality show personality than you can as a taxi driver, farmer, mechanic, teacher, hotel chambermaid, coal miner, auto worker, nurse, home health aide or shipping clerk, work itself is devalued. A decline in the work ethic and an increase in a sense of alienation become inevitable. I hasten to add that this not a new phenomenon caused solely by capitalism. Throughout history a minority of people whose "work" was often unnecessary (if not downright useless) have lived well while the majority of people, whose work was necessary, have lived poorly.

Back in the 1960s the economist Robert Theobald stated that that, given our technological capabilities, it would only take ten percent of the American people to produce all the goods and services the country needed. In the 21st century we are a hundred times more technologically capable, so my version of Theobald's statement is that if everyone worked cooperatively we could produce all the socially useful goods and services we require while working far fewer hours per week than the current 40, 50 or more hours that most of us work at present.

In the plainest English I know, I am saying that if everyone from 16 to 105 years of age put in something like (for the sake of argument) 16 hours a week, we could produce all our food, housing and clothing, and also take care of our health care and educational needs. I included people up to 105 because I believe the best way to stay young and healthy is to keep active. However, I pride myself on being a reasonable person, so for someone 105, I am willing to consider suitably less taxing work and fewer hours. As for the 16 hours of cooperative work per week, while it is an arbitrary figure and used only for illustrative purposes, I didn't simply pluck it out of thin air. I looked at:

- The number of government employees in federal, state, county and city agencies needed to administer programs, such as food stamps, welfare, unemployment insurance, student loans, subsidized housing, and all the other band-aid programs that capitalism needs to keep itself from imploding that will be unnecessary in a utopian society;
- The even larger number of unemployed people, including those who have long since dropped out of the labor force and are not even counted as unemployed;
- The many non-violent people in prison that could safely be released to become productive citizens,

to say nothing of freeing up for useful work all the
people required to keep them in prison;

- How modern technology could be used, not to
increase profits but to decrease the amount of time
people had to work;

- Last but not least—and the largest number of
all—people presently working in occupations that
produce nothing of real value.

If we lived in a society not motivated by mindless
materialism and consumerism, countless numbers of
people would be freed to produce the public goods and
services we actually need.

As part of this cooperative effort to produce public
goods and services, I see nothing wrong in drafting
high school youngsters, 16 and 17 years old, to spend six
months in each of their junior and senior years working
in age-appropriate socially useful work. These six-month
stints would be 40 hours a week as opposed to the
(arbitrarily proposed) 16 hours. I would also suggest that
at 18 all (and I do mean all) our youth serve two years in
the armed services. Their two years of service would also be
full-time as opposed to 16 hours a week. This service would
be a combination of military training and assignments
producing public goods and services. While I think this
national draft would be "good" for our young people, I
don't see why at some time or other everyone shouldn't do
a stint in a work brigade, a kind of Public Service National
Guard. Tasks that require short bursts of societal energy,

such as picking farm crops at harvest time and rebuilding areas hit by natural disasters, come immediately to mind.

I also envision a utopia in which we are cross-trained. Over the course of our lives, we would put in our public service sometimes as farmers, sometimes as mechanics, plumbers or bus drivers and sometimes as workers in health care, education or science.

Since even utopia will require government, I also envision term-limits for holding any political office: two terms and out. In utopia being a politician means you take a few years out of your life to serve as a "citizen politician" and then go back to being a citizen. The same would hold true for all government bureaucrats from secretaries to the heads of agencies that will be needed to manage this planned economy—two years and out. Basically, you would spend two years as a government functionary managing the work that needs to be done and then you would be out and would become one of the "managed."

BANKING, MONEY, AND SCRIP

Republicans, Democrats, liberals, conservatives, independents and all the talking heads are agreed that we need to reduce the deficit and balance the budget. Given my contrarian instincts, my sense is that the problem is not our debt or deficit but our whole monetary system. In *Why Not Utopia?* Therefore, I propose not only a dual social and economic system, but also a dual monetary system: the currency we presently use for the free-enterprise component of utopia and scrip for the utopian component.

Bruce H. Lipton and Steve Bhaerman, in *Spontaneous Evolution: Our Positive Future (and a Way to Get There From Here)* (2009) have given a much better recap than I can of banking, money, and scrip. And since there no possibility that I can improve on what they have written, I will again follow the advice of one of my favorite authors, Anatole France, who said: "When a thing has been said and well, have no scruple, take it and copy it." I therefore offer the reader the following section from the chapter "The Great Banking Robbery," in *Spontaneous Evolution.*

> To understand how completely our society has allowed not only the power of money but the power of the speculative economy to rule, let's take a look at how money got swept into power.

Money has been with us ever since the advent of trade. Gold and other precious metals were pressed into coinage to represent goods that had real value in the world. Instead of having to say, 'I'll give you a twentieth of this goat for that chicken' money became a convenient tool for commerce.'

As merchants accumulated more coins than they could conveniently tote, they began to store the coins with goldsmiths, who issued paper money as IOU's or promissory notes. U.S. currency for example contains the acknowledgement: "This note is legal tender for all debts, public and private."

At some point the goldsmiths made a happy discovery. At any given time, only a small fraction of merchants would come to collect their deposits. Thus began fractional reserve banking, which is the practice of loaning paper money in values up to ten times the actual amount of gold on hand. This practice is a fundamental characteristic of banking systems today.

Loaning money for profit was forbidden under the rule of the church.
However, in the 1500's, after the Protestant Reformation and after King Henry V111

relaxed the lending laws in England, the power of money accompanied civilization on its path into the material realm.

During the next century, the lending policy of loose money followed by tight money, created an economic crisis in England. When loans were plentiful, people borrowed freely and loosely. But at some point, bankers said, "That's enough," tightened their lending practices, and called in their loans. People who had borrowed during good times of economic expansion found themselves unable to pay during times of contraction. Bankers then relieved those unfortunate indebted souls of their collateral, that is, their homes or other property, at pennies on the dollar and then resold the repossessed collateral at a great profit.

War, which is another boon to the bankers, led to the British Crown becoming the world's biggest debtor by the 1600's. But the bankers had a royal solution: create the Bank of England, which in spite of its name, is not part of the British government but a privately held company owned by the bankers themselves.

The Bank of England had a perfect Ponzi scheme, a form of fraud in which belief in the success of a nonexistent enterprise is fostered by quick returns for the first investors from money invested by later investors. The bankers asked the British Government to put up the initial one million pounds. They then loaned out ten times that much—ten million pounds-to their cronies who used this money, made out of thin air, to buy shares in the new bank. The bank agreed to loan the money back to England, securing interest debt with taxes paid by the people.

Meanwhile off in the New World, the economy was thriving. Because precious metals were scarce, the colonialists had been forced to print their own currency, which was called "colonial scrip." This scrip was essentially fiat money, currency backed by nothing more than a commonly accepted agreement that the money had value. Because this money was not debt based but accurately represented the value of goods and services without interest, everyone benefitted. However, a poorly timed boast by Benjamin Franklin squelched that currency and helped hasten the American Revolution.

While visiting England, Franklin was asked how he accounted for the prosperity of the colonies. He credited the issuance of colonial scrip and then added, "We control the purchasing power and have no interest to pay." That's all King George the Third and the Bank of England had to hear.

By 1764, Parliament had passed the Currency Act, which prohibited the colonies from issuing their paper currency in any form. Without the currency to conduct daily business the Colonial economy went into a severe depression. In 1766, Franklin went to London seeking the law's repeal, but to no avail. America's loss of sovereignty over issuing its own currency was a prime cause of the Revolutionary War and a reason why the Founding Fathers were adamant about not having a national bank.

In spite of those good intentions, a battle raged during the first 120 years of America's history over who would be in charge of issuing currency: the banks or the government. As the path of humanity led deeper into materialism, the power of the banks won out. (pp. 168-170)

I would remind everyone that, like the Bank of England, the Federal Reserve is a private banking club. I suggest that:

First, we take back the banks from the bankers and run them for our own benefit;

Second, we create a new monetary system based on utopian scrip which, as with our current U.S. currency, will contain the acknowledgement, "This note is legal tender for all debts, public and private";

Third, while the free-enterprise component of utopia will be free to retain our current paper money, such money will not be backed by the government as legal tender for all debts, public and private. As for the 16 trillion dollar deficit (or whatever the amount we will owe by the time we achieve utopia), my preference is to simply transfer that debt to the private sector. They ran it up they can pay it down. However, even though the debt is primarily the fault of the capitalist system; the bankers, Wall Street, hedge fund honchos, financial speculators, corrupt and incompetent politicians, to default on the debt would irreparably harm millions of ordinary people. Therefore, utopia really should honor the obligation.

What utopia can do is work out equitable arrangements with all those private, corporate, and governmental bondholders to pay down the deficit with utopian scrip and at the same time place a sales tax on all private-sector commercial activity, using that money from the sales tax to pay ourselves back for honoring the obligations we got stuck with.

WAGES AND TAXES IN UTOPIA

According to the Republican platform, and I quote: *prosperity is the product of self-discipline, work, savings, and investment by individual Americans . . . . it provides the means by which individuals and families can maintain their independence from government . . . . and build communities of self-reliant neighbors . . . . it is also the means by which the United States is able to assert global leadership . . . and . . . makes possible our military strength and is critical to our national security.* Throw in reducing taxes and cutting regulations and all is well in their world.

The Democrats, on the other hand, favor good jobs with good pay and are opposed to poverty, which they propose to reduce in half over the next ten years. Somehow, it seems to me that taking ten years to reduce poverty, and then only by half, doesn't speak well for their sense of urgency.

It should be stated up front that utopia will require wage and price controls. Everybody will receive, for the sake of argument, $75,000 per year in utopian scrip for their time spent in socially useful work. My assumption is that this should be enough to purchase everything they need, with $25,000 left over to spend in the private economy. An exception would be that I would not include the high school youngsters and the 18-year-old draftees in the proposed annual rate. I would view that period in their lives as an apprenticeship, as learning useful work habits, and pay them an accordingly different and much lower rate.

Although subject to debate (and I am open to argument), in utopia everyone will receive the same $75,000 per year. As long as the work is socially useful, the remuneration will be the same. It seems to me that we can find other means than money to reward people who work in occupations that require more education, are more useful or more difficult. In the free-enterprise component of utopia we can allow the market to decide how much people earn for their work.

Since even in utopia taxes will be necessary, I will again quote from Washington's farewell address to citizens at the end of his second term: . . . *bear in mind, that toward the payments of debts there must be Revenue, that to have Revenue there must be taxes; that no taxes can be devised, which are not . . . inconvenient and unpleasant . . .*

Because utopia is essentially a faith-based movement (albeit a secular one), it seems only appropriate that we borrow the religious practice of tithing to support one's faith. Since everyone will be earning a living wage, even if not exactly the same wage as everyone else, we can replace all the current cumbersome and unfair tax policies with a flat ten percent tithe. This will have the added benefit of doing away with the IRS bureaucrats collecting (and auditing) taxes, the politicians spending time legislating loopholes, and the lawyers and tax consultants finding those loopholes; which is not be hard for them to do since they paid the politicians to put them in the tax code in the first place. Again, the more we do away with these jobs that are only made necessary by capitalism, the more people we will have available for useful work and the less we will all have to work.

The Role of Free Enterprise in Utopia

Simply put, free enterprise will be allowed to function in utopia. The pre-conditions are that everybody puts in 16 hours (again, this is an estimate) of socially useful work. All private commercial transactions will take place after the individual's obligations to utopia have been fulfilled. In utopia a sales tax will be levied on every private-sector transaction, whether it is a mom-and-pop operation or a corporate conglomerate. The amount of the tax will be determined annually by whatever political structure utopia adopts as its form of government. The sales tax will be used (a) to pay down the deficit or, more accurately, repay utopia for paying down the deficit and (b) to pay the private sector's fair share of everything that utopia has built that the private sector benefits from: roads, bridges, tunnels, transportation networks, energy grids, etc.

Before the private sector gets too upset I would note that their profits would not be taxed; utopia will be content to take what it is entitled to and not one penny more.

Anyone wanting goods and services not available from utopia, wanting extra income or wanting to become rich and own lots of material things will either have to start a business or work for someone who has a business. Starting a business in utopia is virtually risk free since by virtue of putting in your socially useful work you will never go hungry, homeless or without a decent standard of living. An added benefit is that since people choosing to work in the private sector are already assured of life's basic necessities, capitalism will lose its leverage to underpay or overwork them. In fact, utopia may give workers the upper hand in negotiating wages and working conditions.

That being said, if the private sector wants to cheat each other, exploit each other, cut corners to increase profit margins, so be it. The operating principle of the utopian government toward the free-enterprise sector will be *caveat emptor* and don't look to us to bail you out if things don't work out well. On the other hand, if Adam Smith is right and the invisible hand of the market benefits all, then it is a win-win situation for everybody. Utopia can guarantee a life free from the stress of economic insecurity and the private sector can indulge your every wish for as many material things as you want.

The key to a successful utopian and free-enterprise coexistence is for utopia to build an economy of abundance based on people working cooperatively and the private sector behaving in an ethical manner. Whether either of those dreams is possible is problematic, but we will never know unless we try.

PART 4

Imagining Utopia

Would It Be So Terrible If We All Lived Well?

WHAT MIGHT BE

In 1933 President Franklin Delano Roosevelt said, "I see a nation one third ill housed, ill clothed, and ill fed."

Today I see a nation one third in poverty, one third one pay check away from poverty, one third unemployed, one third overworked, and two thirds stressed out. My arithmetic may not be so good but I stand by my analysis. Given our stage of technological development, there is no reason why we can't create an economy of abundance for all. We should have no problem

- Growing all the food we need and feeding everyone;
- Building all the housing we need and housing everyone;
- Manufacturing all the clothing we need and clothing everyone;
- Providing quality health care for everyone;
- Providing free, quality education to every child from pre-K to graduate school as well as continuing education for anybody who wants to continue learning;
- Building all the roads, trains, planes, cars, busses, bridges, tunnels, and mass transit systems we need. You name it we can do it.

We should even be able to develop a leisure society that leaves everyone enough spare time to realize the dream of The Declaration of Independence that among our unalienable rights are, "life, liberty, and the pursuit of happiness." To create this utopian society all that is necessary is to work cooperatively toward those goals and think outside the box into which the Republican Party, the Democratic Party, the media, pundits and conventional wisdom have locked us.

I keep coming back to my uncertainty that people will work cooperatively for the common good, but as the saying goes, today is the first day of the rest of your life—and this is a utopian program.

Health Care

As far back as I can remember, those of us who fought for a universal health care system did so under the slogan "Health Care Is a Human Right." Fairly recently, Lawrence O'Donnell, MSNBC host of "The Last Word," changed that to "Health Care Is a Human Necessity." A difference of only one word, but I think a very significant one.

The Republican Party health care platform is a model of disingenuousness. Sometimes words are strung together just because they sound good. Sometimes they simply make an assertion totally bereft of either facts or context. Sometimes a proposal appears in one sentence and a totally contradictory proposal appears somewhere else.

> *Republicans support the private practice of medicine and oppose socialized medicine in the form of a government-run universal health care system. . . . Medicare patients must be free to add their own funds, if they choose, to any government benefits, to be assured of un-rationed care.*

Hundreds of paragraphs later, they get back to Medicare and Medicaid. Following their own logic, they should call for the repeal of both programs but settle for promising to fix them. Of course, in the above quote they did say they are opposed to a government-run *universal* health care system. You could argue that Medicare is only for the old and Medicaid only for the poor, so they're not universal. On the other hand, at the rate America is going, the old and the poor will soon be damn near universal. And to be fair to the Republicans despite their program's stated intention to fix Medicaid and Medicare (or as they prefer to call it Obamacare) they actually do keep trying to kill both those programs.

My favorite sentence is the one that says people need to be free to add their own funds to any government benefits to be assured of un-rationed care. No matter how I read that sentence, it comes out that if you're too poor to add any funds, the hell with you. If the Republicans have to choose between raising taxes, giving up a tax cut, or leaving the poor to fend for themselves, guess which one they're going to choose.

I again quote from Anatole France, who said, "The law, in its majestic equality, forbids the rich as well as the poor to sleep under bridges, to beg in the streets, and to steal bread." I would re-phrase that to read: The Republicans in their majestic indifference to reality would equally permit the poor as well as the rich to purchase un-rationed care from their own funds.

Reading the Democratic Party's health care plan, I counted enough platitudes to sink a battleship. Here are some of them:

- Our nation faces epidemics of obesity and chronic diseases.
- Half of all personal bankruptcies in America are caused by medical bills.
- The American people understand that good health is the foundation of individual achievement.
- [We favor] savings through competition, choice, innovation, and higher quality care.
- Health care should be a shared responsibility between employers, workers, insurers, providers and government.
- End insurance discrimination.
- [Provide] portable insurance and meaningful benefits.
- Achieve long-overdue mental health and addiction treatment parity.
- Families should have health insurance coverage similar to what Members of Congress enjoy.
- [We support]prevention and wellness . . . a strong health care workforce . . . the elimination of disparities in health care among minorities, American Indians, women and low-income people.
- Make our health care system culturally sensitive and accessible to those who speak different languages.
- Support Public Health and Research.
- Fight HIV/AIDS in our country and around the world.
- Invest in biomedical research and stem cell research.

- Empower and support older Americans and people with disabilities
- We oppose the current (G.W. Bush) Administration's consistent attempts to undermine a woman's ability to make her own life choices and obtain reproductive health care, including birth control. We will end health insurance discrimination against contraception.

Whew! And that wasn't even the whole set of platitudes, nor were they considerate enough to list them the way I did; they just put them all in one paragraph that went on and on until your eyes glazed over. As I noted earlier I am convinced that whoever wrote the Democratic platform was charging by the word.

Clearly the Democrats are against mean-spirited Republicans and for anything and everything that provides everybody with affordable, quality, health care coverage. Since I am also against mean-spirited Republicans and for anything and everything that will provide everybody with affordable quality health care, I agree with the Democrats. However, it strikes me that if the Republicans never met a social program they like, the Democrats never met a simple solution they like when a lengthy, mind-numbing set of platitudes is available. As long as we have poverty, racism, sexism, a "me first" ethos, and the entire range of social ills currently plaguing us, we will not "fix" the health care system—even if Republicans develop a conscience and Democrats learn to how to keep it simple.

I would argue that it is difficult, if not impossible, to live in a dysfunctional society and not be alienated from your own body and that the best fix for our health care system is a healthy society. For anybody out there who thinks health care should be reserved only for those who have money, I offer the following story:

An old guy in Miami Beach, shabbily dressed, goes to an expensive heart surgeon, who determines that the old man needs surgery. But since he is obviously poor, the surgeon says to him, "You know I am the most expensive surgeon in Miami Beach." The old man says, "Fine." The operation is a success. The doctor presents his bill and the old man says, "I'm a poor man, I can't pay this." The doctor reminds him, "I told you I'm the most expensive surgeon in Miami Beach," to which the old man replies, "I know. But when it comes to my health, nothing is too good for me."

Build a utopian society and we will probably "fix" at least half of our current health care problems. As for those problems that just building a healthy society can't fix, all we need to do is (1) find the collective will to provide single-payer health care for all and we'll save 30 percent of the cost of providing health care; (2) eliminate the insurance companies, which serve no purpose other than to add a middleman's cost to health care and we'll save another 30 percent; (3) get rid of all the paperwork that has no relationship to the actual provision of health care and we'll reduce the cost by another 30 percent; (4) eliminate the army of lobbyists, consultants, accountants, lawyers and bureaucrats living off the health care system and we'll get another 30 percent in cost reduction; (5) take away the profit motive and we'll take away the incentive for fraud and waste in every area from over-testing, to over-referring, and over-prescribing, so we can throw in yet another 30 percent.

We can then take the 150 percent (!) we just saved and forget about single-payer or any other payer system and create a utopia in which health care is free; it is part of the social contract—in return for performing socially useful work you receive the health care you need.

And while we're at it we can also set up easily accessible health care clinics in every urban, suburban and rural area; elevate the role of primary care physicians from doctors who mainly prescribe to doctors who mentor their patients and serve much as life-coaches, encouraging their patients to pursue the path of wellness. We can give them fewer patients and enough time per visit to follow the advice of Plato, who said, speaking to the doctors of his day, when treating a slave prescribe with authority and brook no questions, but when treating a free man, discourse with him on the nature of his illness and take no action until he is persuaded of the rightness of the course of action.

We can also extend the above limits on patient-to-doctor ratios to all medical and health care practitioners and providers, creating a working partnership between all providers and patients.

I come back to my central theme, create a utopian society that fosters a decent standard of living, an ethical way of life, and the leisure time to enjoy it and, for most people, good health will follow. I also suggest we stop treating the body as if it were only a machine and combine the best of modern medicine with a holistic approach. I see no reason to exclude nontraditional / nonconventional / non-Western practices from our attempts to stay well. In utopia the health care clinics we set up should offer everything from exercise equipment and programs, to meditation, to tai-chi (to name just three). As the old man said, "When it comes to my health nothing is too good for me."

As someone who wouldn't be here if not for by-pass surgery, who couldn't type these words if not for cataract surgery, who has undergone back surgery and a hip replacement and who takes eight different medications daily, I am merely suggesting that in utopia we provide ourselves with the best of many health care approaches.

EDUCATION

Both the Democratic and Republican Party platforms list a dazzling array of issues they promise to address. If any child, parent, teacher, or administrator is lacking something, the respective platforms are sure to mention it along with a commitment to fix it.

For the Republicans this means: Building on the basics, especially phonics . . . measuring by testing . . . ending social promotion . . . merit pay for good teachers . . . classroom discipline . . . parental involvement . . . strong leadership by principals . . . classes for boys only or girls only . . . home schooling . . . restoring the civic mission of the schools as envisioned by the founders . . . English first as opposed to divisive programs [I assume "divisive" means bi-lingual] . . . choice in education . . . vouchers and tax credits for faith based and charter schools . . . energetically assert the right to voluntary prayer and equal access to school facilities for religious purpose . . . . replace "family planning" programs with increased funding for abstinence education—There was more, but pretty much in the same vein.

The Democratic Party platform is just as long and matches the Republican platform platitude for platitude. What is interesting are the few things omitted that the Republicans included and the few things included that the Republicans didn't mention. The Democrats support transitional bi-lingual education and embryonic stem cell research and, unless I missed it, there are no references to prayer in the schools, abstinence education, vouchers for faith-based schools, home schooling, or classes for boys and girls only.

What I find totally disingenuous about both party planks is the emphasis on educating our youth for the good-paying jobs of the future as the way to end poverty. Education will not end poverty. Poverty is caused by unemployment, part-time employment, and low wages. If we want to end poverty, all it takes is a socio-political decision to guarantee everyone employment at a living wage.

Let me ask you to conduct a simple thought experiment. Let's assume: (1) that every child goes to school, studies hard, gets good grades, goes to college and graduate school and is educated in math, science, and every subject necessary to prepare them for the well-paid jobs of the future, and (2) that there are hundreds of occupations with those well-paid jobs in computers, science, medicine, law, education, finance and so on. Can we then assume that since every child is educated for these high-paying jobs, poverty will be eliminated? Let's look at the probable outcomes.

There probably will not be a need for all those good-paying jobs. We may very well wind up with a surplus of well-educated people who will be unemployed, underemployed or working at McDonald's, Walmart or in any of the other hundreds of occupations that leave you poor while working. We could wind up with the best educated poor people in the world and lots of them.

On the other hand, let's assume that all of those well-educated people do, in fact, find well-paid jobs. What then? I assume they will spend their discretionary income on all kinds of conspicuous consumption and leisure activities. They will shop, travel, stay at hotels, eat out, hire nannies and servants, utilize car washes, taxis, landscapers, and so on. If that is the case, then educating our way out of poverty will simply increase the demand for people to fill all those low-paying jobs, and those jobs will then increase exponentially.

Since all of our people will be fully employed, it seems safe to assume that the people filling those positions will undoubtedly be illegal immigrants or, more politely, "guest" workers. As long as there is a seemingly inexhaustible reservoir of Third World people desperate to trade the grinding poverty of home for the marginally better poverty here, I am sure we will manage in one way or another to allow them to enter the country.

Thus, far from eliminating poverty through education we will perpetuate it and probably even increase the number of poverty-level people. Of course, since these will not be "our" people living in poverty, I guess they don't have to be counted.

Before I propose a utopian educational program, let me comment on the concept of a public school educational system for our children. I don't think we ever had a public school system and we certainly don't have one now. What we have are

- Publicly-funded schools;
- Charter schools (also publicly funded, but selective);
- Private schools;
- Various Christian denominational schools; as well as Catholic, Jewish, Muslim, Afro-centric, and any number of other essentially non-public schools;
- Home schooling;

By way of background for the above assertion, I would note that the early colonists taught their children at home or hired a tutor if they could afford one. Catholics in America had established schools as far back as the 1600s, as did the Puritans. However, it was the Puritans who pointed out the need for public education. Both groups taught the basics—reading, writing and arithmetic—but both also used the schools to reinforce their core religious and social values

After the Revolution, Thomas Jefferson saw the need for a public education system and proposed that tax dollars be used to fund it. He was ignored and it took almost 100 years before public schools came into existence, but only in communities that could afford them. The concept of free and compulsory education for all children started in Massachusetts in 1852 but it was not until 1918 that all American children were required to attend at least elementary school. Of course "all" did not mean that poor children—and blacks, particularly in the states of the former Confederacy, where racial segregation was mandated by law—received anything like the education afforded the children of the wealthy. And the process continues to this day, with college and graduate schools increasingly unaffordable, not just for the poor but even for the middle class.

The first mass exodus from the public school system occurred in the 1840s, 1850s, and 1860s, when the Catholic Church, whose children were often going to public schools, found itself unable to reform what it saw as the blatantly fundamentalist Protestant tenor of the public school system. It established (or, perhaps more accurately, re-established) its own public school system. I believe it is fair to say that the fragmentation process I have described continues to this day; in fact, it may be more pronounced today than in earlier years.

I am not minimizing the difficulties in creating one public school system in a country as diverse and divided as ours. Nor do I underestimate the dangers of trying to emulate our Puritan and Catholic forebears and create a public school system with a single set of core values. However well-intentioned those values may be, conformity was, is, and always will be a serious threat to critical thinking and intellectual freedom. Nevertheless, a public school system seems to me to be a necessary foundation if we are ever to become a *United* States of America.

To repeat my earlier statements, let's provide our children with free public education from pre-K to graduate school and while we're at it, let's throw in free adult continuing education. Let's view education as a life-long process for the enrichment of the individual and society and not simply a path to well-paid jobs.

Let's also move from a rote learning way of teaching, which is essentially passive, to a learner-centered approach that fosters creativity, critical thinking and learning by doing.

If I had my way, schools would be open from 6 a.m. to midnight seven days a week. Children would be able to start school at three months and go any time during the open hours. Learning would always be in session from pre-K to graduate school and beyond. In utopia, continuing education for all would be a way of life from infancy to the day before departing one's earthly existence.

The proposed remedies for our failing education system—the 3 R's, phonics, discipline, rote learning, accountability, merit pay, more homework, continuous testing—may sound good but are not the answer to our educational problems. In fact, I am certain they are part of the problem, not part of the solution. Putting one teacher in a room with 20 or 30 children and compartmentalizing teaching by subject matter ensures that critical thinking, creativity and learning-by-doing will not happen.

Jean Piaget, the Swiss developmental psychologist, said the work of the child is play. So, let's provide our infants and young children with a 1:3 teacher-to-child ratio and a playful environment and start them on the path to creativity while the window of learning is wide open. In elementary and middle school, let's provide a 1:7 ratio so that teachers have enough time to give each child the individual attention she or he needs. In high school, let's use the same 1:7 ratio but enlarge the class size to 49 with one head teacher and enough assistant teachers (or seven co-equal teachers) to maintain the 1:7 ratio. This would give our children the benefit of both personal attention and opportunities to interact within a group large enough to function as a social community.

To those who say we need great teachers and that just putting bodies in a room isn't sufficient, I would say, "What good is all our technology if we don't use it?" You can put an absolutely great lesson, or series of lessons, on television, computers or whatever the latest technology is, and classroom teachers throughout the country can work with that material. Even with "canned" material they can provide all the teaching, mentoring, guidance and encouragement that children need to thrive. I am not suggesting that "canned" material replace live classroom teaching, simply that they can peacefully co-exist.

Finally, placing young people from elementary school through high school in a classroom setting for hours on end strikes me as totally ignoring everything we know about child-hood development. We can, and should, arrange our schools so that children can run, jump, play, exercise, and learn at their own individual pace. If this means they go to school at eight in the morning and finish up at nine in the evening, as long as they are being fed and their parents know where they are, I see no problem. And if we really love our children as much as we profess, we will build our schools with acres of space for indoor and outdoor physical activities to foster the development of a strong and healthy mind-body connection.

In utopia we would accept the concept that it takes a village to raise a child. This means socializing children from early infancy though the formative years to help them grow into caring, productive, and responsible members of the community. To those who say it is the responsibility of the parent to raise the child, I would say that I see no contradiction between the village and the parent raising the child: all I see is synergy.

So, first, let's stop scapegoating teachers and unions and then let's give the village—the teachers—everything they need to be successful.

Then, let's give parents every bit of support they need to be successful parents; specifically, a living wage and a work week short enough so that they can work and still have ample time to spend nurturing their children.

AGRICULTURE

Considering how the family farm has long been idolized in American life, I am absolutely amazed at how few paragraphs both the Republican and Democratic Party platforms devoted to agricultural policy.

The Republican plank reads: floods, bad weather, and escalating fuel costs are a problem . . . farmers need a Farm Savings Account to manage risk . . . since 98% of the 2 million farms are owned by individuals or family farming partnerships we affirm our opposition to the death tax . . . we oppose heavy handed environmental mandates . . . and to meet the surging demand for food and fuel the USDA must remain the leader in agricultural research and the U.S. government should end the mandates for ethanol and let the free market work.

I have no idea how the Republicans figured that any of the above represents a serious farm policy, although I am fascinated that the party of less government wants the USDA to remain the leader in agricultural research.

For their part the Democrats offer platitudinous feel-good sentences that meander all over the place: rural America is home to 60 million Americans and the agricultural sector is critical to the rural economy . . . we depend on those in agriculture to produce [our] food, fiber, and fuel . . . in return we will provide a safety net . . . a disaster relief program . . . expansion of research and an emphasis on trade . . . economic development in rural and tribal communities by investing in green energy . . . [and] address the challenges faced by public schools in rural areas . . . including forest county schools.

<u>Full disclosure</u>: When I graduated from high school in 1947, it was my intention to write the Great American Novel. I decided the first step would be to forego college and work on a farm. After that I intended to ship out with the Merchant Marine, work on some oil rigs, and then hitch-hike around the country until I reached Alaska, by which time I figured I should be ready to write my novel. After working six months on a farm, getting up at 4 a.m., milking by hand, plowing by horse, and finishing up around 8 p.m., I decided the second step should be to go to college.

I am aware of, although certainly not an expert on, such current issues as sustainable farming, local farming, genetically modified foods, organic farming, the environmental dangers of raising farm animals in industrial farms, and the potential for roof-top city farming and similar techniques to boost agricultural production. However, I have no hesitation in saying that the first step in creating a utopian farm policy should be to discontinue the agribusiness method of farming. Instead, we should create throughout the country millions of small-scale family farms that practice sustainable agriculture. My desire to create millions of family farms is not based on nostalgia or a romantic desire to return to a long-ago past. I believe this plan would offer the following benefits:

(1) Creating millions of family farms would diversify our agricultural base, ensuring that crop failures for any reason would be localized and would not have an impact on the whole country. (It's called not putting all your eggs in one basket.) In the same vein, health disasters, from mad cow disease to salmonella outbreaks, would have less of an impact and be easier to control.

(2) Locally grown food reduces the energy needed for transportation and storage, usually tastes better, and might even be more nutritious than much of the produce now available to us. This is not to say that we shouldn't import food from or export food to other countries or other sections of our own country, when they or we are unable to grow foods that are "out of season" or unsuitable for cultivation in a given area.

(3) Diversifying our agricultural base will also certainly allow us to better adapt to whatever climate changes we may face.

If we take away the distortions caused by the profit motive that undergirds the agribusiness, we should be able to come up with a sensible, sustainable agricultural policy, on everything to do with growing and raising the plant and animal food necessary for our survival. We could, for the sake of argument, cut our beef consumption in half and pay ranchers twice as much per pound. Their standard of living would remain unchanged and the environment would probably be better off with half as many cattle. Cutting our meat consumption in half would leave our cost for meat at the dinner table unchanged and, as an added benefit, we would probably be healthier for it. We could even raise cattle on grass, as opposed to corn, if the operating principle was to do what's good for the cattle, the rancher and the consumer, not how quickly we can get the cattle to market to maximize profit.

To carry this a bit further, we could stop commercial fishing, say for five years, and give the fish stocks time to replenish themselves. We could substitute farm-raised fish and, again with the profit motive off the table, we could make sure that the farms are as environmentally safe as our knowledge permits. A moratorium on commercial fishing is not something we can impose on all the countries that engage in it, but it strikes me as something worth thinking about.

Consistent with the concept of utopia having a "mixed" economy, farmers would own their own farms, but by rationally planning annual farm production goals, utopia could eliminate both overproduction of "high cash value" crops and underproduction of "low cash value" crops.

Assuming all the risks associated with drought, floods, tornados and other natural disasters and thereby taking all the insurance profit margins out of that aspect of farming and using the "social labor" of the community to repair any damage, utopia could insulate farmers from the effects of natural disasters. Employing the high school youngsters mentioned earlier and having them spend their two semesters of socially useful work living and working with a farm family, would provide that family with additional support. For our young people, learning the value of work and that food is not grown in a supermarket will be a valuable lesson. Youngsters already growing up in farming families could have the option of remaining on the family farm or living with a city family while performing age-appropriate, socially useful work in an urban setting. Using the 18-year-old draftees and some of those performing their two-week National Public Service stint in farm-related activities would make it possible for farmers to have a life-style consistent with the rest of society.

Will there be farmers who game the system? Will there be farmers who produce less than others yet enjoy essentially the very same utopian benefits as those who work harder or smarter? Perhaps. Will there be situations where, for whatever reason, a significant portion (say 70%) of a given crop is destroyed? Yes. And if utopia tries to ration the remaining 30% in order to distribute it fairly at a controlled price, will human nature take over and create a black market scramble to profit from the shortage? I suppose so. All I can say in defense of utopia is what I stated in my introduction: All solutions are, by definition, imperfect, incomplete and lead to a new set of problems.

Shelter and Clothing

As nearly as I can make out, the Republican Party platform's solution to the housing crisis is to establish a mortgage finance system based on competition and free enterprise, promote personal responsibility by the borrower, rely on private capital, and reduce Fannie Mae and Freddie Mac in size and scope.

For the Democrats, basically their view is that irresponsible lenders tricked people into buying homes they couldn't afford, and their solution is that the President is committed to creating an economy in which home ownership is an achievable dream for all Americans.

I couldn't find any mention of clothing in either of their respective platforms. I guess that's because we get almost all our clothing from China and they didn't want to remind us about all those manufacturing jobs being shipped overseas.

As for providing ourselves with shelter and clothing, we can build all the new housing we need and manufacture all the clothing we need quite easily. The problem is not money, lack of it, our debt or the deficit. The problem is that we have so few people with the necessary work skills and so little appetite for working together for the common good. All that is needed to build all the housing and manufacture all the clothing we need are the necessary raw materials, and those we have in abundance. We can even build the housing and make apartment renovations in an environmentally friendly and energy-reducing way—complete with solar energy, energy-saving appliances—and even include lots of parks and green spaces.

To emphasize the point: money is simply a mechanism to get people to work for the things they need. Money doesn't cut down trees; make wood or bricks; build furniture; produce cotton, wool or synthetic fabrics; or manufacture the machines used to convert those raw materials into houses and clothes. People do.

The problem is that we lack the cultural ethos of cooperation. If we had that ethos, we could just as easily use toothpicks as our current form of money or, better yet, a handshake. We could even develop a social consensus that any work I do for "you" that does not directly immediately benefit me will be repaid by you at some later date. It's called reciprocity and it requires trust in one another—something that may not be possible even in utopia but will certainly never happen under capitalism.

PART 5

Which Side Are You On?

Which Side Are You On?

On June 16, 1858, Abraham Lincoln, speaking at the Illinois State Republican Convention to kick off his campaign for the U.S. Senate, said:

> If we could first know where we are and whither we are tending, we could better judge what to do and how to do it. . . . A house divided against itself cannot stand. I believe this government cannot endure, permanently half slave and half free. I do not expect the Union to be dissolved—I do not expect the house to fall—but I do expect it will cease to be divided. It will become all one thing, or all the other.

In fact, Lincoln was wrong. In 1861, the Union was dissolved, restored later only by force, and today the house is still divided.

To frame Lincoln's statement as a question for today it would be: Can a government endure permanently that is half well-off and half poor, half conservative and half liberal and divided not just by race but by virtually every social and economic issue? The quick answer is "yes," since we've been that way from our earliest beginnings, and the house is still standing.

In the chapter on building a utopian society, I took it as a given that a capitalist free-enterprise system and a socialist utopian planned economy could co-exist. The more relevant question is: Can a house as divided as ours ever find the collective will to become "one nation," let alone create a utopian society?

In the introduction, I stated that all generalizations, by definition, are at best inaccurate and at worst misleading. Since this is my book, I figure I'm entitled to grant myself a waiver and will cheerfully proceed to generalize.

The current divide in America is often characterized as a conservative-liberal divide. I believe this does not capture the full extent of the divisions in our society. Conservatives range from moderate to right-wing authoritarian. Liberals range from moderate to left-wing radical.

To complicate matters, there is another group: true believers. While true believers can be conservatives or liberals, my sense is that they come mainly from the ranks of authoritarian conservatives. To further complicate matters, true believers come in two groups: those willing to die for their beliefs and those who prefer to kill others whose beliefs they dislike. I believe our history makes it abundantly clear that this latter group comes almost entirely from the ranks of authoritarian conservatives.

I am well aware as I write these words that leftists, from the very inception of our country through the Vietnam war years and continuing to today—e.g., when protesting the World Trade Organization or economic injustice—have also used violence. Nevertheless, there is a fundamental left-right divide. The leftists who engage in violence are basically raging against and attacking the state and state institutions, but they rarely attack individuals. Authoritarian conservatives, on the other hand, rage mainly against groups and individuals who threaten their beliefs. Thus their violence includes murdering everybody from abortion providers to gays, lesbians, blacks, Jews, Muslims and communists (and when no communists are available, liberals will do). Their violence is qualitatively different from the violence of the left.

I think it is important to distinguish between the conservative person and the conservative position. It is entirely possible to be a warm, kind, generous, loving friend, spouse, father, have a Ph.D. in anything from the humanities to nuclear physics, and yet work in the public arena for policies that are not just anti-democratic but truly horrific. Likewise, I distinguish between the liberal person and the liberal position. It is entirely possible to be cold, aloof, a lousy friend, a cheating spouse, an absent father or a crooked politician, and still work in the public arena for programs that advance the cause of human freedom.

For conservatives, there is a virtually unbroken line from the establishment of our country to the present on economic justice, civil rights, personal sexual freedom, women's rights, health care and education. Whatever constricts those rights they are for and whatever expands those rights they are against. When they do give ground, it is grudgingly and, usually, only when they have found another group or position on which they can fixate their anger and opposition. I offer one example to support the above hypothesis. I believe that racism is receding—and, as I noted earlier, not nearly as quickly as conservatives fear or liberals would like to believe—but that there is a direct correlation between conservatives' acceptance of the changing racial landscape, however grudgingly, and the energy they now expend opposing gay rights and same sex-marriage. The lyrics may change but the melody lingers on.

It has been noted that whenever two groups, such as conservatives and liberals, are in conflict, the group with the most social cohesion will win. Again, continuing to generalize, conservatives exhibit a large degree of social cohesion around a set of core beliefs:

> Supremacy of God, country and family.
>
> Free enterprise is good.
>
> Any form of socialism is bad.
>
> Small government is good.
>
> Hard work and self-reliance are good.
>
> Government handouts are bad.
>
> Gun control is unconstitutional.
>
> Same sex marriage violates God's law.
>
> God has ordained man as the ruler of the household—albeit he is expected to be benevolent.

As for liberals, their acceptance of the capitalist economic system prevents them from developing a set of alternative core values and all too often reduces them to trying to ameliorate, rather than get rid of, the fundamental inequalities inherent in capitalism. I find it ironic that conservatives, who believe in "rugged individualism," march almost in lockstep on their core values, and liberals, who believe in "community," have difficulty marching together, and certainly not in lockstep, on almost anything.

Whether socialist movements in America have failed because they go against the grain of human nature or the pull of thousands of years of Western cultural development, or whether our divisions of race, class and gender are simply too great to overcome, are open questions. However, creating a utopian society out of this unfriendly soil is, to put it mildly, a daunting task.

If you ask conservatives if they would like to live in a utopian society, they will never give you a straight "yes" or "no" answer. They will tell you that it won't work, that it has failed everywhere it has been tried, that some people will do all the work and others will do nothing because there is no incentive to work hard, and so on. If you say "I know you think it won't work for the reasons you just gave but if it could work, would you like to live in a utopian society?" they still won't answer "yes" or "no." They understand very clearly that if they say, "yes" the next question will be "Do you have any ideas on how we might get there?" And since they don't want to get there, they are not likely to let themselves be trapped into that discussion.

Throughout our history, liberals have attempted to build a new and better day. In 1913 there was a general strike of silk workers, mostly women, in Paterson, New Jersey. In December 1911, The American Magazine had published a poem by James Oppenheimer, titled "Bread and Roses," which was subsequently set to music by Caroline Kohlsaat. The song was adopted by the women in the 1913 strike and sung on the picket lines and at rallies; in fact, the strike itself became known as the "Bread and Roses Strike."

> As we go marching, marching, in the beauty of
>   the day,
> A million darkened kitchens, a thousand mill
>   lofts gray,
> Are touched with all the radiance that a sudden
>   sun discloses,
> For the people hear us singing: Bread and
>   Roses! Bread and Roses!
> As we go marching, marching, we battle too for
>   men,
> For they are women's children, and we mother
>   them again.
> Our lives shall not be sweated from birth until
>   life closes;
> Hearts starve as well as bodies; give us bread,
>   but give us roses.
> As we go marching, marching, unnumbered
>   women dead
> Go crying through our singing their ancient
>   call for bread.

Small art and love and beauty their drudging
    spirits knew.

Yes, it is bread we fight for, but we fight for
    roses too.
As we go marching, marching, we bring the
    greater days,
The rising of the women means the rising of
    the race.
No more the drudge and idler, ten that toil
    where one reposes,
But a sharing of life's glories: Bread and roses,
    bread and roses.
Our lives shall not be sweated from birth until
    life closes;
Hearts starve as well as bodies; bread and roses,
    bread and roses.

The strike failed.

In 1931, coal miners in Harlan County, Kentucky, were locked in a bitter and bloody struggle with the mine owners. J.H. Blair, the local sheriff, and his deputies, hired by the mining company, went to the home of union organizer Sam Reece in an attempt to intimidate him. Reece had been warned in advance and escaped, but Blair and his men simply proceeded to terrorize his wife Florence and their children. After they left, Florence Reese wrote the song "Which Side Are You On." Below is one verse.

> They say in Harlan County
> There are no neutrals there
> You'll either be a union man
> Or a thug for J.H. Blair

The strike failed.

Since then, while many strikes have succeeded, over the years the pattern has been that the gains made by working people in one era are rolled back in another era as capitalism consistently demonstrates its ability to bend but not break. And I would add that this process, of gains followed by a rollback, has been and is true for blacks, Jews, women, gays, Muslims—any group that has been oppressed or discriminated against. Without a fundamental shift in power, any and all gains can be snatched away at a moment's notice either by the corporations when it suits their purposes or by the government when the political winds change.

We have been and continue to this day to be a nation of the powerful and the powerless, of the privileged and the underprivileged, of those who have and those who have not.

A new day, a better day, has yet to come. For those who want to see that day, the question is: Any ideas on how to get there and how willing are you to commit to trying to make that day a reality?

SOME CLOSING THOUGHTS

I believe once something is written, it takes on a life of its own independent of the author's intent, background, or life history. If I were 21 rather than 83; six feet, five inches rather than five feet, five inches; never married or, as I am, married for 60 some years; religious or not (as it happens, I'm not); manic or depressed (I'm neither), the words in Why Not Utopia? once committed to paper would speak for themselves. Whatever meaning I intended is completely out of my control and entirely dependent on the meaning the reader attaches to the words. However, since most people like to know something about the author, following are a few remarks to provide a context for how I came by my ideas.

Because of the Depression back in the 1930s, my parents sent me to live in the country with an aunt and uncle from the time I was three until I was ten. While living with them in Rockland County, New York, I spent one of those years, when they were living in a particularly small town, in a one-room country schoolhouse. My memory is that the school was right out of "Central Casting" for an America that is now almost completely gone. Before entering the classroom, we boys had to line up to get our knuckles rapped with a ruler just in case the teacher missed some misbehavior later on. He must not have missed much, because my memory is that my knuckles were rapped all day long. His idea of education included corporal punishment for talking in class, squirming in one's seat, getting low test marks, failing to submit homework on time, teasing girls, and for other mysterious and unexplained infractions that he saw no need to explain.

At the same time, my aunt and uncle, who were both members of the Communist Party, introduced me to children's books very different from those I was reading in my one-room schoolhouse. As young as I was, I was introduced to communist ideas. I was also introduced to the Spanish Civil War, the fight for black equality and women's rights, Paul Robeson, and folk singers such as Woody Guthrie, Huddie Ledbetter (Leadbelly), Josh White, Burl Ives and countless others.

Looking back it doesn't surprise me that with that early background I joined the Communist Party when I was about 19 and stayed in it for about four years. In 1953, I was living in Flint, Michigan, and was called before the House Un-American Activities Committee (HUAC), chaired, in Flint by Representative Kit Clardy. According to a Wikipedia account, Clardy's conduct of the hearings "not only abused the witnesses but incited violence against them." His conduct of the hearings also "contributed to the lynch spirit which swept the city. A number of workers were dragged from their jobs in automobile plants by lynch gangs and beaten; hostile witnesses were evicted from their homes; their families had to go into hiding to escape the fury of mob hoodlums . . ."

I was one of those workers and was eventually forced to leave town and start life over. As it happened, by the time the committee came to town I was already disenchanted by the Communist Party's slavish devotion to the Soviet Union and its concomitant failure to connect to "the masses." I announced at that time to one and all that I was going to take a ten-year sabbatical from politics and do some serious reading and thinking about everything that needed serious reading and thinking. Although I did go to Dr. King's 1963 March on Washington and did occasionally march to protest the war in Vietnam, basically, I spent the next 50 years reading and thinking. So I guess it is safe to say that it was a long ten-year sabbatical.

The reason I was in Flint was that in 1949 the Communist Party put out a call for students (I was at what was then Oswego State Teachers College) to quit school and go to work in factories in major industrial cities. My memory is that I went to a meeting at Cornell University and, swept up in the euphoria of the moment, I promptly quit college and wound up in Flint. There is a funny, and sobering, sequel to my youthful enthusiasm. Years later I ran into one of the student organizers of the event. "I went to Flint," I said. "Where did you go?" It turned out he had gone to graduate school. But by then I already knew the term "apparatchik," so I was not too surprised. Nor am I surprised today by our own pseudo-patriots who are prepared to fight America's wars with someone else's sons and daughters.

What I came to realize during my years of reading and thinking was that even though I was raised by an atheist aunt and uncle, they actually raised me in a church: the

Communist Party. We had our own sacred texts: Marx, Engels, Lenin, Stalin and Mao. We had our own infallible leaders—granted they were changed with regularity, but they were infallible while in leadership. We had our true believers, who rationalized every twist and turn handed down from on high; our keepers of the faith, who excommunicated heretics; our apostates, whom we reviled and vilified; and our faith-affirming rituals.

If nothing else, the experience and my subsequent readings left me in awe of the power of faith—whether in God or man's perfectibility—to enable some true believers to risk their lives for their faith, some to kill others whose faith they don't like, and some to remain absolutely closed to any ideas that might threaten their faith.

As for me, I remain true to my faith that a better world is possible, but based on the empirical evidence, skeptical that our species will ever get to that better place. However, it strikes me that trying to get there is far better than not trying.